AFFORDABLE HOUSING

DESIGNING AN AMERICAN ASSET

AUTHORS

Adrienne Schmitz Urban Land Institute **Washington, D.C.**

Suzanne Corcoran Corcoran Jennison Associates **Alexandria, Virginia**

Isabelle Gournay University of Maryland at College Park **College Park, Maryland**

Matthew Kuhnert National Building Museum **Washington, D.C.**

Michael Pyatok Pyatok Architects, Inc. **Oakland, California**

Nicolas Retsinas Director, Joint Center for Housing Studies, Harvard University **Cambridge, Massachusetts**

Jason Scully Urban Land Institute **Washington, D.C.**

This book is published in conjunction with the exhibition *Affordable Housing: Designing an American Asset,* presented at the National Building Museum, Washington, D.C., February 28–August 8, 2004.

Guest Curators: Ralph D. Bennett, Jr., and Isabelle Gournay
Chief Curator: Howard Decker
Director of Exhibitions: Catherine Crane Frankel
Curatorial Associate: Matthew Kuhnert
Exhibition and Graphic Design: Chester Design Associates

ULI Project Staff

Rachelle L. Levitt
Executive Vice President, Policy and Practice, Publisher

Gayle Berens
Vice President, Real Estate Development Practice

Adrienne Schmitz
Director, Residential Community Development,
Project Director, Author

Jason Scully
Senior Associate, Policy and Practice, Author

Nancy H. Stewart
Director, Book Program

Barbara Fishel/Editech
Manuscript Editor

David James Rose
Associate Editor

Recommended bibliographic listing:
Schmitz, Adrienne, et al. *Affordable Housing: Designing an American Asset.* Washington, D.C.: ULI–the Urban Land Institute, and the National Building Museum, 2005.

ULI Catalog Number: A20
International Standard Book Number: 0-87420-940-4
Library of Congress Control Number: 2005900689

Photo Credits:

Front cover, clockwise from top left:

©Brady
Steinkamp/Ballogg Photography, Inc.
Faleide Architects, PC
Todd and Associates, Inc.
Pugh + Scarpa
Urban Design Associates

Back cover, left to right:

Daniel Solomon
Everton Oglesby Architects
Anton Grassl
David Baker + Partners
Steve Hall © Hedrich Blessing

Affordable Housing: Designing an American Asset has been generously supported by the following:

Benefactor

Patrons

Fannie Mae Foundation

R REALTOR
NATIONAL ASSOCIATION OF REALTORS ®

NP NIXON PEABODY LLP
ATTORNEYS AT LAW

Related **Capital Company**
Capital Solutions

Supporters
Bank of America
Century Housing
National Association of Home Builders

Contributors
Corcoran Jennison Companies
Council of Federal Home Loan Banks
Horning Brothers
Meridian Investments, Inc.
National Council of State Housing Agencies
National Housing Trust
National Leased Housing Association
Newman & Associates, Inc.
Reznick Fedder Silverman
U.S. Environmental Protection Agency

Associates
Affordable Housing Tax Credit Coalition
Bruner Foundation
Crawford/Edgewood Managers, Inc.
Homes for America, Inc.
Housing and Development Reporter
Institute for Responsible Housing Preservation
The John Stewart Company
Katz & Korin, PC
Local Initiatives Support Corporation
National Foundation for Affordable Housing Solutions
National Housing Conference
Neighborhood Reinvestment Corporation and the
  NeighborWorks® System
Southern California Housing Development Corporation

The National Building Museum gratefully acknowledges the U.S. Department of Housing and Urban Development, Fannie Mae Foundation, and NATIONAL ASSOCIATION OF REALTORS® for their additional support for the traveling exhibition of *Affordable Housing: Designing an American Asset.*

Honorary Committee
The Honorable Christopher S. Bond
The Honorable Barney Frank
The Honorable John F. Kerry
The Honorable Barbara A. Mikulski
The Honorable Michael G. Oxley
The Honorable Jack Reed
The Honorable Paul S. Sarbanes
The Honorable James T. Walsh
The Honorable Anthony A. Williams

Advisory Committee
Emily Axelrod, Bruner Foundation
Louis Borray, U.S. Department of Housing and Urban Development
Juanita Britton, D.C. Department of Housing and Community Development
Simeon Bruner, Bruner Foundation
Henry Cisneros, American CityVista
Suzanne Corcoran, Corcoran Jennison Companies
Chuck Edson, Nixon Peabody LLP
Conrad Egan, National Housing Conference
David Engel, U.S. Department of Housing and Urban Development
Alan Hirmes, Related Capital Company
Stanley Jackson, D.C. Department of Housing and Community Development
Marty Jones, Corcoran Jennison Companies
G. Allan Kingston, Century Housing Corporation
Jeffrey Lesk, Nixon Peabody LLP
Robert Reid, Center for Housing Policy
Stephen Ross, Related Capital Company
Anthony Schuman, New Jersey Institute of Technology, School of Architecture
Daniel Solomon, Solomon E.T.C.
Vickie Tassan, Bank of America, Inc.

About ULI–the Urban Land Institute

ULI–the Urban Land Institute is a nonprofit education and research institute that is supported by its members. Its mission is to provide responsible leadership in the use of land in order to enhance the total environment.

ULI sponsors education programs and forums to encourage an open international exchange of ideas and sharing of experiences; initiates research that anticipates emerging land use trends and issues and proposes creative solutions based on that research; provides advisory services; and publishes a wide variety of materials to disseminate information on land use and development. Established in 1936, the Institute today has more than 24,000 members and associates from more than 80 countries representing the entire spectrum of the land use and development disciplines.

About the National Building Museum

The National Building Museum, created by an act of Congress in 1980, has a mission to explore the world we build for ourselves—from our homes, skyscrapers, and public buildings to our parks, bridges, and cities. Through exhibitions, education programs, and publications, the Museum seeks to educate the public about American achievements in architecture, design, engineering, planning, and construction.

A private, nonprofit organization, the Museum is supported by contributions from individuals, corporations, foundations, associations, and public agencies.

ACKNOWLEDGMENTS

This book, published in conjunction with the exhibition *Affordable Housing: Designing an American Asset*, is the result of collaboration among many individuals and organizations, without whom this project would have been impossible.

The museum is especially grateful to the those, who contributed to this thoughtful overview of how affordable housing is enhanced by good design. Henry Cisneros, Suzanne Corcoran, Michael Pyatok, and Nicolas Retsinas developed insightful commentaries that demonstrate that well-designed developments can indeed offer new desirable housing for the least-wealthy Americans and yield encouraging opportunities for our communities.

For the design of both the catalog and exhibition, many thanks are due to Patricia Chester, principal of Chester Design Associates. Supported by Dina Spoerl and Holly Schroat, her vision has given the subject matter elegance and excitement, and has brought a vivid sense of clarity to a topic that is oftentimes difficult to grasp.

This book is published in collaboration with ULI–the Urban Land Institute, and the museum extends its grateful appreciation for its vital role in its production. We would like to thank executive vice president Rachelle L. Levitt and vice president Gayle Berens for their guidance throughout the project, as well as book program director Nancy H. Stewart, associate editor David James Rose, and manuscript editor Barbara Fishel for their excellent work. The museum is especially indebted to the expertise and support of project director Adrienne Schmitz and senior associate Jason Scully, whose hard work and dedication made this publication possible. Additional thanks are extended to Alex Bond for compiling the glossary, and John Rodrigues and David Takesuye for their contributions to the case studies.

The museum also gratefully acknowledges the contributions of guest curators Isabelle Gournay and Ralph Bennett, Jr., for their cooperation and expertise in developing *Affordable Housing: Designing an American Asset*. Their assistance was crucial to the success of the project, and their support and dedication are much appreciated.

At the National Building Museum, we are grateful for the work and support of our many colleagues. Chase Rynd, president and executive director, enthusiastically endorsed this endeavor and saw it through to its completion. Howard Decker, chief curator, was crucial in the development of the project and has provided consistent support for both the exhibition and the publication. Catherine Crane Frankel, director of exhibitions, superbly managed the logistics and kept the project on budget and schedule while providing encouragement. Stan Watters, vice president for development, along with Essence Newhoff, director of development for exhibitions, and Troy Patterson, sponsorship manager, ably coordinated efforts between sponsors and the museum. The logistics for the traveling exhibition were managed and coordinated by the out-standing efforts of Shelagh Cole, traveling exhibitions manager, and Carolynne Harris-Knox. Dana Twersky, collections manager, masterfully coordinated the loan and donation of objects. Hank Griffith, exhibitions coordinator, with Chris Maclay, exhibitions preparator, and MaryJane Valade, exhibits designer, made significant contributions to the design, fabrication, and installation of the exhibition. Jayson Hait masterfully edited the exhibitions script and contributed many ideas that were critical to its content. Dedicated researcher Joan Mathys provided invaluable contributions to this project above and beyond what was expected, for which we are most grateful. We would also like to thank curatorial assistant Matthew Fitzsimmons for his eager enthusiasm and energy.

We would be remiss for not mentioning our peers and friends, Deborah Sorensen and Michael R. Harrison, for their counsel and suggestions.

Finally, this book could not have been completed with-out the data and photographs supplied by the developers, housing authorities, and architects responsible for the projects presented here. Their cooperation and support were much appreciated.

Matthew Kuhnert
Curatorial Associate
National Building Museum

One of the fundamental tenets of the National Building Museum is that design matters, and that good design can have a range of benefits beyond its obvious aesthetic value. This is true at all scales, whether an urban plan, a community library, or even a humble cooking utensil. It is certainly true with respect to housing, where clever planning can yield a more livable and convenient arrangement of spaces, thoughtful material choices can reduce energy consumption, and well-conceived details can create a sense of specialness that truly makes a house a home. Unfortunately, many people believe that such high-quality residential design is a luxury available only to some members of society.

This book, developed in cooperation with ULI–the Urban Land Institute and based on an exhibition developed by the National Building Museum, refutes that notion. It eloquently demonstrates that low-cost housing need not be of poor quality—in fact, it can be an asset to the community of which it is a part. Architects and developers across the country are now producing a variety of single- and multifamily residences that are comfortable, attractive, and easily maintained, while still being affordable to a broad spectrum of American families. The projects presented here are diverse in geographical location and architectural expression, reflecting a range of financial, political, and design strategies that may provide valuable lessons for others seeking to enhance the quality of life in their own communities.

Creating affordable housing is quite challenging—local building codes, neighborhood skepticism, and technical constraints, for instance, can make it a slow and frustrating endeavor. It is hoped, however, that this publication will encourage architects, developers, public officials, and others to consider innovative approaches to sheltering citizens in precarious economic circumstances. And if those readers who are fortunate enough not to worry about housing costs find some ideas in these projects, well, that's fine, too.

Chase W. Rynd
President and Executive Director
National Building Museum

Richard M. Rosan
President
ULI–the Urban Land Institute

TABLE OF CONTENTS

Everyone needs a place to call home. When night falls, every person confronts the basic need for a place that is safe, decent, and restful, a place to stow one's possessions, to clean up, to recharge for the challenges of the next day. These are basic human needs that require the physical space we call home, whether for a night or a lifetime. The form that a home assumes can vary—rented or purchased, homeless shelter or entry-level house, public housing or move-up home, urban or suburban, central city high rise or rural manufactured house. But the need for housing within the reach of every person is an American priority.

Tragically, for a growing number of families in our country, finding affordable housing seems impossible, reaching crisis proportions in many communities. When I served as Secretary of Housing and Urban Development in the Clinton Administration, our greatest challenges were housing affordability, homelessness, and the conditions in public housing across the nation. As a developer of workforce housing, I continue to work on those problems today. It is clear that rental housing, a stepping stone to homeownership, must be made more affordable. Many families today are spending more than half their income on rent—a level of expenditure that doesn't leave families enough money for food, transportation, clothing, and medical essentials. Homelessness remains a serious problem, with children making up a growing share of the homeless population. HOPE VI, which has helped to turn crumbling public housing developments into thriving mixed-income communities, is under attack. Funding is being reduced once again and in 2005 the program will have funds for only six grants to meet pressing redevelopment needs in hundreds of cities.

The national challenge is immense. It is a hopeful sign that in cities and towns across the country, governmental agencies, nonprofit organizations, architects, home-builders, and other community builders are coming together to produce more and better affordable housing. The projects described in this book show what is possible when creative and dedicated people work together. They assemble multiple funding sources often including grants, loans, tax incentives, and private capital. They design homes that are economical and easy to maintain, reflecting the traditions of surrounding communities.

This book and the companion exhibition, *Affordable Housing: Designing an American Asset*, document 18 affordable housing developments that embody design excellence and provide homes in which people of modest means can live with dignity. The developments were selected by the National Building Museum to reflect the diversity of solutions to the problem of housing affordability. Initially displayed at the National Building Museum, the exhibition has already focused national attention on both the problems and the potential solutions. Now the exhibition is traveling across the nation so that more Americans can reflect on the basic national agenda of affordable housing for all people. I sincerely hope that readers of this book will come to understand the pressing human need and will lend their efforts to bring high-quality affordable housing to every American.

Henry Cisneros
Chairman and CEO, American CityVista

AFFORDABLE HOUSING

DESIGNING AN AMERICAN ASSET

Affordable Housing: Designing an American Asset features 18 recent projects that represent affordable and pleasant places to live. They come in all styles, sizes, and funding arrangements and range from urban to rural locations and from single-family detached homes to group residences for those with special needs. The projects were selected because they successfully address the following issues:

1   Logical and productive land use;
2   Clear accommodation of activities, from public to private;
3   The use of buildings to separate active public spaces from quiet private spaces;
4   A focus on the unique qualities of each place in the project;
5   The dwelling unit's amenities, flexibility, and ability to personalize it.

The United States faces a crisis in affordable housing. Prices rise steadily, and construction does not keep pace with the urgent need. More than 14 million American households spend more than half their income on housing. The vast majority of those households are at the bottom fifth of the income distribution. Some 6.3 million households receive rental subsidies, but of them, about 3 million still pay more than 30 percent of their income for housing.

Since 2000, prices of for-sale homes have risen four times faster than incomes, and rents have risen three times faster. The very poor are experiencing the worst housing problems, but working-class households—fire-fighters, teachers, janitors, police officers—are also affected. Many are being priced out of the communities they serve.

Many studies point to a widening gap in the availability of affordable housing. Those who provide affordable housing—whether through federal programs, state or local agencies, nonprofit developers and community development corporations, or for-profit developers—all strive to make the financial details of each project workable, but doing so is extremely difficult. Most projects require some kind of subsidy, but housing is only one of many needs competing for a shrinking pie. The 2002 report from the federal Millennial Housing Commission recommends increasing expenditures in almost every existing federal program, along with reorganizing some. Some advocates believe that better alternatives exist than federal appropriations, including the creation of trust funds, local tax incentives, and policy solutions such as inclusionary zoning. Proactive federal, state, and local policies can and must help to create adequate supplies of well-designed affordable housing that improves the quality of life for individuals and their communities. Every citizen should be able to pursue and achieve the American Dream: a safe, sound, and attractive place to call home.

ISABELLE GOURNAY

Since the 1800s, governments at all levels have worked to improve housing standards for the health and welfare of the nation's residents. In the 19th century, regulations for apartment design required that rooms have windows, permitting access to daylight and ventilation. Later, the Great Depression prompted massive federal action to meet the critical housing shortage. Following World War II, waves of urban renewal often misguidedly cleared thousands of acres of homes to build high-density, low-income dwellings. Slums, tenements, concrete high rises, filth, crime, and racial segregation often were the result of these efforts. For many residents, the American Dream had become a nightmare. Today, some of these icons of past efforts are being razed to accommodate more humane alternatives. Mixed-income smaller-scale infill developments are providing attractive, safe housing in settings that foster pride. But in other cases, the homes created by early initiatives still remain, providing housing of last resort for those with no options. The following narrative details the history of affordable housing in the United States.

HELPING THE "DESERVING POOR"

I n the 19th century, private citizens, guided by egalitarian ideals, were the primary advocates and providers of affordable housing. Some entrepreneurs built cottages in company towns to keep their workers content, productive, and nearby. With the Progressive Era, expertise began to replace morality.

Family in poverty gap, New York City tenement room, ca. 1889.
Jacob A. Riis, photographer
Library of Congress

House in Graniteville, South Carolina, 1848.
Library of Congress

1848

1848

In Graniteville, South Carolina, William Gregg sets the precedent for textile mill company towns by building model cottages for his workers.

1854

In *Homesteads for the City Poor,* advocate Joseph Tuckerman writes in favor of decentralized single-family homes over dense city living. Suburban relocation becomes a topic of heated debate among reformers.

The Model Lodging House Association is founded in Boston and builds efficiently planned and well-built apartment units with a 6 percent return on investment.

1864

The New York City Citizen's Association Council on Hygiene inaugurates an efficient campaign to improve and enforce housing and sanitary standards.

1867

New York City passes the Tenement House Act, the first comprehensive law to supplement legal construction standards. Revisions to the act in 1901 establish minimum requirements for ventilation, lighting, and allocated space. Although enforcement is limited, other cities widely replicate its clauses.

1889

Jane Addams founds Hull House in Chicago, Illinois. It is modeled after English settlement houses and promotes neighborhood reconstruction. Women begin playing important roles as reformers, researchers, and administrators in the uphill battle for better housing.

1890

Reporter and photographer Jacob Riis publishes his landmark book, *How the Other Half Lives: Studies among the Tenements of New York,* convincingly arguing that the path to better housing is through environmental reform.

1892

Financed by Congress, the Commissioner of Labor begins a national study of slums. Two years later, compelling statistics are published only for Baltimore, Chicago, New York, and Philadelphia.

1894

In his article, "The New York Tenement-House Evil and Its Cure" in *Scribner's Magazine,* architect Ernest Flagg condemns housing on narrow lots and advocates "scientifically planned" block housing centered on large courtyards.

Washington Sanitary Improvement Company apartment house
Washington, D.C., ca. 1897.
National Archives and Records Administration

1895

The Department of Labor publishes *The Housing of the Working People*, the first major government-sponsored study of poor Americans' living conditions.

1896

The Octavia Hill Association is founded in Philadelphia to improve the housing conditions of the working class.

1897

The Washington Sanitary Improvement Company (WSIC) is founded as a business philanthropy. WSIC and the Washington Sanitary Homes Company, founded in 1904, build well-planned apartment units that match the design and scale of rowhouses in the nation's capital. Although reasonable, rents are not within reach of most alley dwellers.

1901

The revised New York City Tenement House Act is passed and becomes a model for regulatory laws across the nation.

1902

The McMillan Plan to redesign the monumental core of Washington, D.C., in commemoration of the capital city's centennial ignores the burning issue of alley dwellings.

1908

Sears, Roebuck & Co. publishes its first *Book of Modern Homes and Building Plans.* Mail-order models start at $650, including plans, specifications, and materials.

1913

Deductions on mortgage interest payments are instituted at the same time as the Individual Income Tax Law.

1917

First federal intervention. An emergency situation—finding living quarters for workers in war industries and their families—prompts Congress to pass the first legislation in American history that allows federal spending on housing for private citizens. A new division of the Labor Department, the U.S. Housing Corporation, builds 6,000 single-family homes and 7,000 apartment units.

Congress establishes the U.S. Shipping Board to oversee Emergency Fleet Corporation (EFC). EFC helps build 8,800 homes in 23 cities.

In the 1920s, suburban bungalows and garden apartments provided the middle class with reasonably priced, well-designed shelter, but living conditions for the poorest Americans still needed to be improved. Congress and the federal government saw no reason to interfere with the market economy, but a few states and cities ventured into creative funding legislation. The disastrous effects of the Great Depression on building activity led advocates for publicly subsidized housing to join forces under the aegis of the National Public Housing Conference, National Association of Housing Officials, and Labor Housing Conference.

Garden Homes Cooperatives, Milwaukee, Wisconsin, 1924.
Paul Jakubovich, photographer
City of Milwaukee, Department of City Development and Historic Preservation Section

1919

Economist Edith Elmer Wood publishes
The Housing of the Unskilled Wage Earner: America's Next Problem.

Milwaukee Mayor Daniel W. Hoan proposes the creation of public housing corporations with stocks owned by local governments and private citizens, leading to formation of the Garden Home Company. Tenants have the opportunity to purchase their homes at below-market prices, about $5,000.

1921

Milwaukee's first large-scale housing project, Garden Homes, is built.

California passes the Veteran's Farm and Home Purchase Act to facilitate homeownership for veterans.

1926

Coppertown, Utah, is a late example of the company town. State-of-the-art Craftsman bungalows are rented to employees.

1927

The New York State Limited-Dividend Housing Companies Act allows 20-year tax exemptions for corporations and restricts their profit to 6 percent, enabling Jewish workers' cooperatives to flourish in the Bronx.

Garden Homes Cooperatives, Milwaukee, Wisconsin, 1923.
City of Milwaukee, Department of City Development and Historic Preservation Section

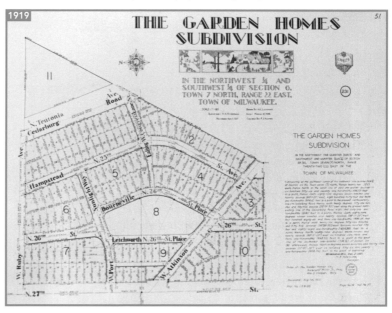

Coppertown, Utah, ca. 1926.
Utah State Historical Society

1930

Journalist Catherine Bauer attends Ernst May's seminar, "Frankfurt's Course for New Construction," which showcases that city's much heralded housing program. Her book, *Modern Housing*, published in 1943, influences many progressive architects and reformers.

Amalgamated Dwellings is built in New York City's Lower East Side tenement district. Designed by Austrian architect Roland Wank, the brickwork is as distinguished as that in "Red Vienna."

1931

Settlement worker Mary Simkhovitch and social worker Helen Alfred establish the National Public Housing Conference (renamed the National Housing Conference in 1950).

Sponsored by Herbert Hoover, the President's Conference on Home Building and Home Ownership makes recommendations to improve home financing and lays the groundwork for many initiatives adopted during the following decade.

1932

Alfred Kastner, Oscar Stonorov, and William Pope Barney design the Carl Mackley Houses in Philadelphia, Pennsylvania. Construction takes place in 1934 and 1935. The Full Fashion Hosiery Workers Union sponsors the homes and receives loans for 85 percent of the cost from the Housing Division of the Public Works Administration.

The Emergency Relief and Construction Act authorizes the Reconstruction Finance Corporation to make loans to corporations established to provide low-cost housing and to reconstruct blighted areas.

1933

The Home Owner's Loan Act creates corporations that are allowed to refinance distressed homeowners' mortgages.

The National Industrial Recovery Act authorizes federal funds for slum clearance, low-cost housing, and subsistence homesteads. It creates the Public Works Administration, whose Housing Division is allowed to provide loans to limited-dividend programs.

As construction activity hit rock bottom, federal legislation established an institutional framework for housing reform. A major first step was the passage of the National Housing Act in 1934, which created the Federal Housing Administration (FHA) to stimulate longer-term mortgage financing. Government intervention provided employment and addressed urban blight. Because loans by the Public Works Administration to nonprofit organizations had not yielded many units, the PWA built its own 21,441 low-rent units in 36 cities.

With the U.S. Housing Act of 1937, housing providers won a major congressional battle: low-rent housing in urban and rural areas and on Indian reservations became a public responsibility. A new agency, the U.S. Housing Authority (USHA), was authorized to lend $800 million to its local counterparts.

War-related factory jobs drew an influx of rural residents into the cities, increasing the need for housing. Signed into law in late 1940, the Lanham Act allowed federal funds to be used to construct public housing for defense industry workers, and more than 700,000 units were built. The government developed temporary communities, some featuring cutting-edge designs by major architects. By 1942, when all government housing activities were placed under the umbrella of the federal Public Housing Authority and directed toward the war effort, USHA units numbered 100,000 and were located in 140 cities.

Ida B. Wells Housing Project, Chicago, Illinois, 1942.
Jack Delano, photographer
Library of Congress

1934

The National Housing Act establishes the Federal Housing Administration and sets minimum property standards for FHA-insured mortgages. The FHA plays a key role in the rebound of the private homebuilding industry and helps expand suburbia and consolidate social and racial divides. Its objective is to broaden the spectrum of home owners by providing government insurance for mortgages made by private lenders.

The Public Works Administration embarks on direct construction of low-cost housing.

Mayor Fiorello La Guardia establishes the New York City Housing Authority, the first municipal housing authority in the United States.

Congress ratifies the creation of an Alley Dwelling Authority (ADA) for the District of Columbia to reclaim slums and provide alley dwellers with sanitary, if spartan, affordable housing. Direct congressional funding is so limited that ADA constructs only 2,800 units by 1940, at a time when Washington, D.C., has an inventory of at least 20,000 substandard units.

1935

The Resettlement Administration is created to combat rural poverty and initiates a subsistence homestead program as well as plans for three Greenbelt towns: in suburban Maryland, Ohio, and Wisconsin.

1936

Initiated by the New York City Housing Authority and funded by the Emergency Relief Administration, First Houses is the first public housing project to open its doors to tenants in the United States. The project combines rehabilitation of existing tenements, demolition and removal, and new construction; preserves commercial activity on the ground floor; and brings greenery to interior courts.

Built in the 1930s, Colonial Village in Arlington, Virginia, is one of the earliest large-scale rental housing projects built under FHA programs and the first to receive federal mortgage insurance. The original 1,000 units are developed on 30 acres.

President Franklin D. Roosevelt notes in his second inaugural address, "I see one-third of a nation ill-housed, ill-clad, and ill-nourished."

Thirty-three states pass legislation allowing cities and counties to establish public housing authorities (PHAs).

The Wagner-Steagall Housing Act is passed, and USHA is created under the general supervision of the Secretary of the Interior.

Catherine Bauer asserts in *Architectural Record* that federally sponsored low-rent housing is not simply a temporary "weapon in the war against the Depression" but "is recognized as a permanent responsibility."

The Bankhead-Jones Farm Tenant Act marks the government's first entry into providing rural housing loans (at 3 percent interest for 40 years).

Subsidies for American Indian housing are instituted. These programs, which cover all financing and operating costs exceeding the renter's payments, are similar to today's Section 8 rent subsidy program. Indian housing authorities can be established by tribal ordinance or by state law.

The Farm Security Administration (FSA) takes over the housing responsibilities of the Resettlement Administration.

"Separate but equal" housing is a New Deal rule, strikingly illustrated by Langston Terrace, a Washington, D.C., low-income rowhouse and garden apartment complex. It is named after John Mercer Langston, a representative from Virginia and the first African American to serve in Congress.

Colonial Village, Arlington, Virginia, ca. 1936–1940.
National Archives and Records Administration

1936

1938

The Federal National Mortgage Association (Fannie Mae) is created to purchase FHA-insured mortgages in the secondary market. Mortgage markets are equalized and standardized throughout the country and made safer for both homeowners/borrowers and investors.

1940

The U.S. Census produces the first comprehensive survey of the country's housing stock.

Delayed by what Chicago's black community denounces as racial discrimination, construction of the Ida B. Wells Homes, a PWA initiative on the city's South Side, finally begins. At completion, the 1,622-unit project exhibits model management and tenant participation as well as superior amenities, including an X-ray clinic and a kindergarten.

Defense Homes Corporation (DHC) is established, and $100 million is appropriated for housing War and Navy department workers. DHC is transferred to the federal Public Housing Authority in 1942.

With the approval of the Lanham Act by Congress, the Public Works Administration is authorized to provide housing at defense and military installations.

Although the private sector finances most of the permanent housing for defense workers, their temporary housing principally draws on public funds. Homebuilders welcome this opportunity to build small, modernized versions of familiar models, and architects experiment with design, as for Aluminum City Terrace near Pittsburgh, Pennsylvania.

The Army accepts the 700 series as the standard building type for barracks and other mobilization camp structures. In less than a year, camp capacity quadruples to accommodate 1.5 million men.

Farm Security Administration architects design war workers' housing in Vallejo, California.

Detail of sculpture at Langston Terrace, Washington, D.C., ca. 1930–1950.
Theodor Horydczak, photographer
Library of Congress

1937

Women gardening in front of Glenn L. Martin
defense housing, Middle River, Maryland, 1942.
Marjory Collins, photographer
Library of Congress

1942

War Time Housing exhibition at the Museum of
Modern Art, New York City, features work by noted
architects Eero Saarinen, Richard Neutra, and
Louis I. Kahn.

Six hundred houses are constructed in six months
for aircraft workers at the Glenn L. Martin Company
outside Baltimore. Martin funds one-third of these
units, and the rest are financed with federal funds.
Skidmore, Owings & Merrill designs the house
plans and uses the Cemesto building system,
so-named for the mix of cement and asbestos
comprising the exterior wallboard siding.

Using the Homasote Company's precision-built
system of prefabricating housing, the firm of Barrett
and Hilp constructs nearly 5,000 homes for shipyard
workers in Portsmouth, Virginia. At one point, they
produce 80 houses a day.

Construction begins on Vanport, Oregon, a
complete city of nearly 10,000 units for Henry J.
Kaiser's shipyard workers and their families.

Levitt and Sons constructs 750 houses in Norfolk,
Virginia, for Naval officers and their families.

Channel Heights housing community in San Pedro,
California, is completed. Designed by Richard
Neutra, it provides housing for shipyard workers.

The first phase of Chicago's Cabrini-Green public
housing project is begun.

1944

In Chicago, the National Conference on Postwar
Housing foreshadows the dilemmas of the following
decade.

Congress passes the Servicemen's Readjustment Act
(G.I. Bill of Rights). Among its provisions are
college education for returning veterans and loans
to buy homes and start businesses. The Veterans
Administration (now the Department of Veterans
Affairs) initiates a home loan guaranty program,
limited to owner-occupied units.

SUBSIDIZED HOUSING AS MASS PHENOMENON

During the post–World War II baby boom, federal legislation and subsidies established a dual-level housing policy that impacts the lives of Americans according to their income. Loans insured by the FHA and guaranteed by the Veterans Administration favored middle-class homeownership and fueled the white flight to the suburbs. Levitt and Sons and other community developers viewed the production of small, low-cost houses as an important and profitable market.

The 1949 Housing Act was a landmark law for rural housing. Expanding the 1937 Farm Tenant Act, it gave authority for rural housing programs to the Farmers Home Administration (now the Rural Housing Service) and enacted a large-scale construction program.

By 1956, public housing authorities managed 424,000 units, or about 1 percent of the nation's ownership housing stock and 2.3 percent of the rental units. Debate over public housing remained heated: private builders and voters frequently challenged and opposed its funding, while architects and housing providers were increasingly aware of its aesthetic and practical shortcomings. Most subsidized housing for the elderly was readily accepted and integrated into communities. Such housing was initially built by nonprofit organizations with government aid; after 1959, public housing authorities themselves assumed the construction.

Levittown, New York, ca. 1950.
Wurts Brothers Photographers
National Building Museum, Gift of Richard Wurts

1945

With the return of veterans and a major population shift to the West, many parts of the country experienced tremendous housing shortages. In addition, construction costs rose rapidly.

President Harry S Truman appoints Wilson W. Wyatt to the position of housing expeditor for the Veterans Emergency Housing program.

1947

The Reconstruction Finance Corporation receives authorization to issue up to $50 million in loans for prefabricated houses and signs a $15.5 million contract with the Lustron Corporation, whose first all-steel house was constructed near Chicago the preceding year.

1949

The total number of homes built since January 1946 reaches 5.1 million.

The National Trust for Historic Preservation is founded.

The National Housing Act of 1949 creates an urban renewal program to support slum clearance and urban redevelopment, expands the public housing program, and establishes rural housing programs under the domain of the Farmers Home Administration.

The Wherry Act, introduced by Senator Kenneth Wherry of Nebraska, authorizes FHA financing for military housing. Such homes, often referred to as "Wherrys," comprise about 1,400 square feet, with a bath and a half.

1950

The private sector and many voters vehemently oppose public housing. Criticism of its aesthetics mounts among architects and housing providers. In March 1950, a referendum on a plan by the Seattle Housing Authority to build 2,600 city-owned units is defeated by a three-to-one vote.

Joseph Eichler, a homebuilder known for his elegant and ultramodern models, offers a starter home at Sunnyvale Manor, California, for less than $10,000. Working with architects Anshen & Allen, Eichler introduces two features that now typify his home design: an orientation toward the backyard by way of a glass wall and an open plan that unites the kitchen, dining, and living areas.

Aerial photograph of Levittown, New York, ca. 1950.
National Archives and Records Administration

1953

Congress investigates an FHA scandal. Unscrupulous builders, aided by corrupt FHA officials, had reaped enormous profits at taxpayers' expense.

Elizabeth Wood resigns as executive director of the Chicago Housing Authority (CHA), having held the post since 1937, because the municipality disapproves her attempts to integrate CHA's properties.

1954

The Free Press in Glencoe, Illinois, publishes *Planning, Politics and the Public Interest: The Case of Public Housing in Chicago*, which analyzes CHA's lost battle to build projects on vacant sites in middle-class districts.

1955

The Capehart Act initiates a privatization program for military housing. Similar to the program under the Wherry legislation, private developers construct the Capehart units. Unlike Wherry, however, the military controls the finished homes and establishes the rent. Capehart houses are larger than Wherrys and include single-family and duplex models. In addition, design parameters focus on maintaining privacy, preserving the natural environment, and integrating homes within the existing military facilities. By the conclusion of the Capehart program in 1964, almost 250,000 Wherry and Capehart units have been built for the military.

1956

The Federal Highway Act launches a major road construction program that encourages many middle-class Americans to relocate to the suburbs and destabilizes many poor urban areas.

1959

Section 202 of the 1959 Housing Act initiates a program for housing for the elderly in which non-profit and limited-profit organizations can benefit from direct government loans at below-market interest rates.

Victoria Plaza, the first public housing project designed especially for the elderly, is built in downtown San Antonio, Texas. Owned by the San Antonio Housing Authority, the nine-story apartment building occupies a 2.36-acre site and includes 185 units.

Victoria Plaza Apartments, San Antonio, Texas, 1958–1960.
San Antonio Housing Authority

As the country turned more progressive, advocacy, legislation, and implementation regained momentum. Title VI of the 1964 Civil Rights Act prohibited discrimination in all programs receiving federal assistance, including housing, while the Fair Housing Act, enacted as Title VIII of the 1968 Civil Rights Act, specifically barred discrimination in the sale or rental of housing. The Department of Housing and Urban Development (HUD) was created in 1965, and its Cabinet-level status gave housing more prominence in the federal government. Public housing authorities were allowed to lease privately owned units. The landmark HUD Act of 1968 authorized mortgage interest subsidies for low-income homeownership and rental housing under the Section 235 and 236 programs. The HUD Act of 1970 provided federal financial support to encourage the creation of new communities with housing for all income levels. To facilitate partnerships between the private and public sectors, cities and states created housing finance agencies.

The pursuit of excellence in design also regained momentum. Through workshops and award programs, housing officials and the architectural profession cooperated to produce alternatives to tower blocks, at once user friendly and "defensible" against criminal activities. Sociological inquiries and "post occupancy" evaluations assessed both successes and failures. To make public housing more affordable to the poorest tenants, the 1969 Brooke Amendment capped rent payments at 25 percent of income and authorized operating subsidies to offset the reductions in public housing authority income. The amendment also tended to make public housing an option of last resort, however, and contributed to its decay.

A segregated apartment project is picketed by pro-integration demonstrators, 1963.
National Archives and Records Administration

1960

The New York State Housing Finance Agency is created.

Construction of the Robert Taylor Homes begins in downtown Chicago. When completed, it is the world's largest public housing development, with more than 4,300 units. According to the Chicago Housing Authority, "By containing a large low-income population on an isolated site, the Robert Taylor property became a national symbol for the errant philosophy of postwar public housing." By 2005, the entire project is slated for demolition.

1961

Public Housing Administration Commissioner Marie McGuire stresses the need for "imaginative design" in public housing.

Financing under the FHA Section 221(d)(3) and 221(d)(4) programs is expanded beyond housing for families displaced by urban renewal to include financing for low- and moderate-income families in general.

1962

The NAACP holds campaigns against discrimination in housing.

President John F. Kennedy signs Executive Order 11063, which outlaws housing discrimination in activities involving the federal government, including financing insured by the FHA or guaranteed by the V.A.

1963

St. Francis Square, designed by Marquis and Stoller in San Francisco, California, wins the Award of Merit in the first FHA Honor Award for Residential Design.

The Public Housing Administration initiates Awards for Design Excellence, with winners to be selected in collaboration with the American Institute of Architects, the American Society of Landscape Architects, and the National Association of Housing and Redevelopment Officials.

1964

The Civil Rights Act is passed.

Passage of the Economic Opportunity Act launches the "War on Poverty."

A total of 605,000 public housing units are under government management.

1965

Congress passes the Department of Housing and Urban Development Act and makes HUD a Cabinet-level department. Programs of the Veterans Administration and those for rural housing, however, remain under the U.S. Department of Agriculture.

Self-Help Enterprises is founded in California's San Joaquin Valley. The nation's first rural self-help housing organization for farm laborers and other low-income families, it leads 4,600 families to homeownership.

1966

The Massachusetts Housing Finance Agency establishes the first state housing program with a clear policy for economic and racial integration. In each development it finances, 25 percent of the units must be made available to low-income households.

The Demonstration Cities and Metropolitan Development Act authorizes $1 billion for HUD's "Model Cities" program (ended in 1974).

HUD initiates a design award program juried by prominent architects and designers that covers such categories as low-rent public housing, low-income housing, FHA-insured private housing in urban renewal areas, and housing for the elderly.

1968

The Fair Housing Act is enacted as Title VIII of the Civil Rights Act.

The Housing and Urban Development Act establishes a ten-year goal of constructing 6 million low- and moderate-income housing units, of which 2.6 million will be built. Also created are the Section 235 interest subsidy program for low-income homeownership and the companion Section 236 program for low-income rental housing. An amendment generally prohibits construction of high-rise public housing projects for families with children.

The Housing Act of 1968 establishes the Government National Mortgage Association (Ginnie Mae) to expand availability of mortgage funds for moderate-income families.

1963

St. Francis Square Cooperative Apartments, San Francisco, California, 1987. Marquis and Stoller, Architects, Claude Stoller

1969

The Brooke Amendment to the U.S. Housing Act of 1937 limits public housing rents to 25 percent of a family's income.

Title I of the National Housing Act authorizes FHA loans for mobile homes costing up to $10,000.

An environmental impact statement is now required for all new federally assisted housing.

1970

The New Community Development Corporation is created within HUD to support the development of new communities that include diversified land use patterns, community facilities, and affordable housing.

New York State creates the Urban Development Corporation.

1972

The St. Louis Housing Authority demolishes three buildings of Pruitt-Igoe, the city's mammoth high-rise public housing development. The following year, the St. Louis Housing Authority confers with HUD, and both agree that the complex is not salvageable. The remaining buildings are razed.

ASSISTED HOUSING AT THE CROSSROADS

Public housing faced a major crisis, and the news media's focus on inner-city pathologies, such as economic and social problems, glossed over the federal government's failure to provide sufficient operating funds and generally ignored thousands of well-managed, livable properties. As their tenants' income declined and maintenance costs and crime increased, several large public housing authorities entered receivership. Decisions to raze entire developments often failed to include provisions for the relocation of tenants and ignored the structures' sound construction and potential historical significance. From eradication to integration, this rocky period laid the groundwork for current urban and architectural trends in affordable housing.

In 1986, Congress enacted the low-income housing tax credit (LIHTC) program, which awards tax credits competitively through the states to private housing providers. This program has become the principal mechanism for preserving and producing affordable housing. In 1990, the HOME Investment Partnerships block grant program was devised to assist state and local governments in providing low-income housing. Intermediary organizations such as the Local Initiatives Support Corporation (LISC) and the Enterprise Foundation were created to assist private providers.

Washington Elms, Cambridge, Massachusetts, c. 1979.
Cambridge Housing Authority

1973

The New York Coalition to Save Housing, Institute for Architecture and Urban Studies, and the New York State Urban Development Corporation design low-rise, high-density housing prototypes.

Citing program abuses, President Nixon pronounces a moratorium on assisted housing.

More than 1 million public housing units are under government management.

1974

The Housing and Community Development Act rewrites the 1937 Housing Act to create the Section 8 housing assistance payments program (now called the housing choice voucher program). The Section 8 program increases low-income tenants' choice of housing and bases the level of assistance on HUD-established fair-market rents. This legislation also creates the community development block grant (CDBG) program.

Montgomery County, Maryland, passes the country's first inclusionary zoning law: in exchange for density bonuses, developers of more than 50 units must make 15 percent of their units affordable, and the public housing authority can purchase a third of these less expensive dwellings.

1976

The U.S. Supreme Court rules in favor of the Gautreaux plaintiffs in their class action suit against the Chicago Housing Authority. It will take 15 years for the CHA to comply with the injunction of relocating 7,100 black families outside their segregated communities.

Millard Fuller establishes Habitat for Humanity International in Americus, Georgia, with the mission of eliminating poverty-level housing worldwide. This nonprofit organization relies on self-help and volunteer sweat equity as families help each other to build their homes.

1977

Congress passes the Community Reinvestment Act.

1979

Michael Svirdoff founds the Local Initiatives Support Corporation, forging an alliance among businesses, foundations, and local community groups.

1980

The Housing Authority of Charleston, South Carolina, initiates an infill housing program for low-income families displaced by gentrification. Respect for traditional house plans (with an open porch or veranda along the side, typical of Charleston) helps promote social integration and maintain the value of adjacent properties.

1981

Chicago Mayor Jane Byrne moves temporarily into Cabrini-Green, one of the city's most crime-ridden public housing projects.

Dade County (Miami), Florida, is authorized to levy a surtax on commercial real estate transfers for housing purposes.

Seattle voters approve a $48.1 million bond issue to construct housing for elderly and disabled persons.

The Cleveland Housing Network is established to rehabilitate vacant and abandoned homes and sell them to low-income families.

1982

James and Patty Rouse create the Enterprise Foundation. Since its inception, the foundation has raised and invested enough money in loans, equity, and grants to create 144,000 low-income housing units.

Coachella Valley Housing Coalition in Riverside County, California, is founded as a nonprofit public benefit corporation to develop housing for those who do not earn enough to buy or rent in the private market. Today, the coalition helps low-income people improve their living conditions through advocacy, research, and the construction and operation of housing and community development projects.

The New York City Housing Partnership is founded and becomes one of the largest producers of affordable housing in the United States.

HUD sponsors an "affordable housing demonstration" in Elkhart, Indiana, the historical center of the mobile home (manufactured housing) industry.

Charleston Infill Housing, Charleston, South Carolina, 1984.
Bradfield, Richards, Rhodes & Associates, Architects, Inc., Atlanta, Georgia

1980

1983

The Boston Housing and Redevelopment Authority holds a design competition among private developers to transform Columbia Point, a public housing project built in the 1950s, into Harbor Point, a mixed-income community completed in 1989.

The BRIDGE Housing Corporation is established in San Francisco. As the state's largest nonprofit developer, BRIDGE creates and manages a range of affordable, high-quality homes for working families and seniors. Collaborating with partners, BRIDGE serves communities by designing housing solutions that create jobs, retail activity, transit access, services, and open space—all ingredients for healthy and sustainable neighborhoods.

The Housing and Urban-Rural Recovery Act begins housing development action grant and rental rehabilitation programs.

1986

Congress enacts the LIHTC program, which awards tax credits competitively through the states to private housing providers. This program has become the principal mechanism for preserving and producing affordable housing.

Seattle voters approve a $12 million bond issue to build 1,500 units for large families on scattered sites throughout the city as a way to integrate affordable housing into existing neighborhoods.

Sandtown-Winchester Townhomes. Baltimore, Maryland, 1982.
© Janis Rettaliata

1982

1987

The Bruner Foundation in Cambridge, Massachusetts, establishes the Rudy Bruner Award for Urban Excellence.

1988

The Fannie Mae Foundation creates the Maxwell Awards of Excellence for the production of low-income housing.

Congress passes the Fair Housing Amendments Act, banning housing discrimination against persons with disabilities and families with children.

1990

The Cranston-Gonzalez National Affordable Housing Act becomes law; it includes several provisions related to special groups such as the elderly and persons with disabilities. It incorporates the HOME investment partnerships block grant program, which assists state and local governments in providing low-income housing, and the AIDS Housing Opportunity Act.

1992

President George H. W. Bush's National Commission on Severely Distressed Public Housing reports that 94 percent of housing developments in the United States provide "decent, safe, and sanitary housing at a reasonable price." The remaining 6 percent, however, "located primarily in deteriorating neighborhoods of large urban communities, [are] plagued by crime, unemployment, and deteriorated physical conditions." The commission further asserts that "traditional approaches to address these problems [are] not working."

Washington Elms, Cambridge, Massachusetts, 1979–1986.
Cambridge Housing Authority

The HOPE VI program (Homeownership and Opportunity for People Everywhere) was developed to revitalize and replace distressed public housing. HOPE VI revitalization usually entails the demolition of existing public housing projects and their replacement by mixed-income developments. Public/private partnerships supported by generous HUD grants finance these activities. The best projects successfully mend the urban fabric and strike a balance between integration and invention in design. The Native American Housing Assistance and Self-Determination Act also represents significant legislation, providing housing block grants to Indian tribes and Indian housing authorities. In 1993, Congress made LIHTCs permanent.

Policies remain volatile in the face of budget crises, economic downturns, and variations in the political landscape. Despite useful recommendations, the 2002 Millennial Housing Commission Report has not yielded any concrete results to date. The Bush Administration would like to convert Section 8 vouchers into state block grants, but the proposal has generated little support.

College Park, Memphis, Tennessee, 2000.
Torti Gallas and Partners

1993

HOPE VI program is created to replace distressed public housing with mixed-income developments.

Architect and Auburn University professor Samuel Mockbee founds the nonprofit Rural Studio, where students design and build environmentally sensitive and user-friendly homes and amenities in Alabama's depressed areas.

1998

The Quality Housing and Work Responsibility Act is enacted to reform the public housing program.

1999

About 3.9 million American families spend more than half their income on housing costs.

2000

The Chicago Housing Authority and HUD sign a five-year, $1.5 billion plan to transform the city's public housing.

America's homeownership rate reaches a new record high of 67.7 percent in the third quarter of 2000. A total of 71.6 million American families own their homes—more than at any time in American history. At the same time, decent housing remains beyond the reach of millions of low-wage workers.

Westbury Neighborhood, Portsmouth, Virginia, 1993.
Urban Design Associates

Bryant "Hay Bale" House, Mason's Bend, Hale County, Alabama,1993–1994.
Photograph © Timothy Hursley

2003

Congress passes the American Dream Down Payment Initiative, administered under HUD's HOME Investment Partnerships program. The act enables eligible low-income families who are first-time homebuyers to receive a maximum down-payment assistance grant of $10,000 or 6 percent of the purchase price of the home, whichever is greater.

2004

HOPE VI program is subject to reauthorization.

Park DuValle, Louisville, Kentucky, 1996.
Community Builders, Inc.

Access to affordable and decent housing is the most prevalent challenge for working American families today. Despite unusually strong income growth in the 1990s, an astonishing 95 million Americans face housing cost burdens beyond their means, or live in crowded or inadequate conditions. In fact, more than twice as many people in the United States face housing problems as lack health insurance.[1]

The U.S. Department of Housing and Urban Development defines "affordable" as housing that costs no more than 30 percent of a household's monthly income. Thus, a worker who earns the current minimum wage of $5.15 per hour should pay no more than $268 per month for rent and basic utilities, an amount that does not cover the rent on a modest one-bedroom apartment in any county in America.[2] Nearly one-third of all households spend at least 30 percent of their income on housing and 13 percent spend 50 percent or more on housing costs.

In addition to problems of affordability, many working families face inadequate housing conditions, or home-lessness. Nearly 2 million households live in severely inadequate units, some lacking such basics as hot water, electricity, or a bathroom. Overcrowding (more than one person per room) remains a problem, particularly among immigrant households. In 2000, 26 percent of immigrant households lived in crowded conditions. All told, more than 6 million households live in over-crowded conditions, the most since 1960. On any given night, about 850,000 people are homeless. Over the course of a year, about 3 million people experience homelessness—nearly 40 percent of whom are children.[3]

Rapid escalation of prices has pushed home prices and rents beyond the reach of many working families. Middle-class families in many metropolitan regions are seeing once affordable housing become unaffordable. The Millennial Housing Commission calculated that it would take production of more than 250,000 units a year for more than 20 years to close the current housing affordability gap.[4]

DEFINITIONS

Housing problems affect low- to moderate-income households across the nation, particularly in high-cost metropolitan areas on both coasts—regions that have seen the largest housing appreciation in recent years. These households are often divided into four categories: those of the extremely low income (ELI), making less than 30 percent of the area median income (AMI); those of the very low income (VLI), making between 30 and 50 percent of the AMI; and low income (LI), making between 50 and 80 percent of the AMI. Moderate-income households are designated as those who earn between 80 to 120 percent of the AMI.

"Workforce housing" is a term that describes housing for those who are generally middle income—earning anywhere between 80 and 120 percent of the AMI. In high-cost areas of the country, these households find increasing difficulty affording decent housing. Teachers, nurses, firefighters, police officers, and other essential workers often fall into this income range. In much of the Northeast and California, these very essential workers have been priced out of the for-sale housing market and even the rental market. The inability of teachers, police officers, and others to find decent affordable housing near their workplace can threaten the long-term economic health of high-cost regions.

GROWING HOUSING CRISIS

Despite rising prices, most Americans are well housed, and in fact, more Americans than ever—68.3 percent—are homeowners. But that figure is substantially lower for minority households. Only 48.4 percent of African American households and 47.4 percent of Hispanic households own their homes. Further, much of the recent rise in ownership can be attributed to historically low interest rates, which have offset some of the rise in prices. As interest rates rise, ownership will likely fall, increasing demand for rental housing. Meanwhile, the supply of affordable rental properties has stagnated in many markets. Nationally, for every three rental units added between 1992 and 2001, two were removed.[5]

Because housing costs and income vary so much by location, national statistics do not reveal the gaps in affordability in certain high-cost regions. In some higher-priced locales, such as Boston, Washington, D.C., and San Francisco, typical apartment rents require more than 30 percent of both salaries of an average working couple. One study of Boston housing points out that in 2002, 43 percent of all renters were paying more than 30 percent of their income on housing and 21.5 percent were paying more than 50 percent.[6]

Household growth is projected to continue at a rapid pace over the next decade, and household growth translates directly to demand for housing. At the same time, many regions are seeing a dwindling supply of buildable land, increasing restrictions on land development, resistance to high-density development, and exclusionary zoning practices, all of which make it difficult for the market to produce any kind of housing, let alone affordable housing. Further, the supply of existing low-cost housing continues to shrink because of physical deterioration on the one hand and gentrification on the other.

Prospects for additional income supports or housing subsidies are equally bleak. As the federal deficit balloons, the calls to cut spending on social and housing programs are growing, even as the need for these programs escalates.

MEETING THE AFFORDABILITY CHALLENGE

Government programs are a critical part of the solution to housing the nation's low- and moderate-income households. But the commitment to government programs has declined and many programs—even effective ones—have suffered funding cuts or elimination. Nonprofits and other organizations provide a certain amount of assistance as well but cannot keep up with the growing need.

Federal Programs

Over the years, the federal government has attempted to provide housing solutions for vulnerable households. The Department of Housing and Urban Development (HUD) directly and indirectly oversees most of the federally sponsored housing projects in the nation. HUD's mission is to increase homeownership, support community development, and increase access to affordable housing, free from discrimination. HUD administers programs such as the HOME Investment Partnerships Program, community development block grants (CDBGs), and HOPE VI, programs that are crucial to stave off further net losses. The HOME Investment Partnerships program has helped to acquire, produce, or rehabilitate hundreds of thousands of rental units. CDBGs provide funds for neighborhood redevelopment projects. Housing accounts for about one-third of CDBG expenditures.

HOPE VI was charged with eradicating severely distressed public housing by redeveloping it as mixed-income communities. Since 1993, the program has awarded more than 440 HOPE VI grants totaling nearly $5.4 billion—and leveraging additional billions—in more than 160 cities, resulting in the redevelopment of thousands of housing units. Continuation of the program is currently in question, and it is likely to suffer considerable funding cuts.

Administered largely by state housing finance agencies, the low-income housing tax credit (LIHTC) program helped to finance approximately 1.4 million affordable rental units between 1987 and 2000. Other federal and quasi-government sources for housing policies and programs include Federal Home Loan Banks, Fannie Mae, and Freddie Mac. These agencies have been important in providing funds and support for affordable and workforce housing programs.

State and Local Programs

States also have their own set of state-sponsored programs, usually offered through a housing board. An example of a state housing agency is the Pennsylvania Housing Finance Agency (PHFA). Typical of state agencies, it was created to provide more affordable housing for older adults, families of modest means, and persons with disabilities. To date, the agency has financed more than 100,000 houses and 56,000 apartment units while saving 32,000 homes from foreclosure.

PHFA's funding comes from a variety of sources, including the sale of its own securities to private investors throughout the United States and program fees and funds that may be passed through from the state or federal government. Agency expenses are paid from fee and investment income, and parts of the investment earnings are used to subsidize housing programs.[7]

Some states and counties also have semi-autonomous housing trusts, which are reserves of funds for affordable housing. The Housing Trust of Santa Clara County in California is a public/private partnership created in 1997 by the Santa Clara County Board of Supervisors, Silicon Valley Manufacturing Group, Santa Clara County Collaborative on Housing and Homelessness, and Community Foundation Silicon Valley. Santa Clara, home to Silicon Valley, is one of the most expensive housing markets in the nation, and the county has had significant problems providing housing for low- and moderate-income workers.

Capitalized largely by the private sector, the trust operates a revolving loan fund (and occasionally provides grants) to leverage funds for affordable housing. The Housing Trust has raised $20 million since it was established in 1999, which will leverage approximately $180 million in development. The trust offers three primary products: 1) predevelopment loans for non-profit developers; 2) gap financing for special projects, typically for the homeless; and 3) buyer assistance for households earning up to 120 percent of the AMI.[8]

Also important are redevelopment authorities that use state, federal, and private money to redevelop neighborhoods and provide affordable housing.

In Virginia, the Norfolk Redevelopment and Housing Authority (NRHA) is one of the oldest such agencies in the nation. It is dedicated to revitalizing downtown Norfolk and has made more than $86.5 million in rehabilitation loans in 19 conservation neighborhoods. To date, NRHA has initiated projects totaling 1,779 acres of redeveloped and affordable housing.[9]

States and localities can also promote affordable housing production by adopting inclusionary zoning programs, which encourage or require residential developers to include affordable units in their market-rate projects as a condition of approval. Montgomery County, Maryland, was one of the first counties to institute an affordable housing mandate, and localities in California, Massachusetts, Colorado, and New Jersey have followed.

Nonprofit Organizations

A vast number of nonprofit organizations nationwide have established programs to increase availability of affordable housing. The Enterprise Foundation is a private, nonprofit foundation that helps America's low-income families in their struggle out of poverty by providing decent homes, access to steady employment, quality child care, and safer streets. Working with a network of 2,500 community organizations nationwide and through its 15 local offices, the Enterprise Foundation has leveraged close to $5 billion in investments and donations to help build almost 160,000 affordable homes and help nearly 40,000 hard-to-employ people find jobs since 1982. In addition to providing funding and working with cities, the foundation offers training and resources for local groups and has an extensive online database of related programs and operations.

The National Low Income Housing Coalition (NLIHC) is another nonprofit dedicated to ending America's affordable housing crisis. The NLIHC policy agenda is organized around five priority areas: preservation, production, public housing, vouchers, and services. Five corresponding policy committees comprising NLIHC members review policy proposals and make recommendations to the NLIHC board of directors on its policy positions.[10]

The Housing Partnership Network is another national nonprofit committed to preserving and creating affordable housing. Its membership consists of 79 regional nonprofits operating in 37 states. The national network attracts funding from major sources such as Fannie Mae; the Ford, Rockefeller, and Freddie Mac foundations; and others. The partnership's mission includes revitalizing neighborhoods, developing and financing affordable rental housing, helping lower-income families become homeowners, and providing an array of vital social services.

Collectively, the members have developed, preserved, or financed 300,000 units of affordable rental housing; built or helped low-income families purchase or rehabilitate 200,000 homes; and provided homeownership counseling to 250,000 low- and moderate-income households. Through the Housing Partnership Network, member organizations gain access to new sources of capital and technical resources, share innovation, and help shape national housing policy.[11]

Another nonprofit, the Local Initiatives Support Corporation (LISC), sponsors the transformation of distressed communities and neighborhoods through resident-led, community-based development organizations. Through providing capital, technical expertise, training, and information, LISC supports the development of local leadership and the creation of affordable housing; commercial, industrial, and community facilities; and businesses and jobs.[12]

The Greater Minnesota Housing Fund is a state-based nonprofit organization that has provided resources to address affordable housing needs in the Twin Cities region. The fund provides technical assistance and investment in nonprofit and for-profit development of new affordable housing, and facilitates the participation of employers, lenders, local officials, and others in affordable housing development. The fund sponsors research on cost-cutting development techniques, and educates and advocates for affordable housing. It runs a multifamily housing development program, a homeownership program, and the "Building Better Neighborhoods—Starter Home Initiative," which promotes creation of economically balanced communities that include affordable starter homes. It also sponsors an employer-assisted housing program and a housing rehabilitation program. The fund's efforts are targeted to households earning 80 percent of the AMI. Since it was created in 1996, the fund has helped produce more than 4,800 affordable housing units.[13]

The Fannie Mae Foundation, the largest foundation in the country devoted to affordable housing, creates opportunities for affordable homeownership and stronger communities across the United States. The foundation supports professional development of public officials and leaders of nonprofits engaged in affordable housing. Fannie Mae supports homeownership education programs and awards grants to nonprofit organizations that create affordable housing.

For-Profit Initiatives

For-profit institutions have been involved in affordable housing efforts, some, for example, by providing subsidized loans or funding for the projects, others by developing affordable housing. Bank of America actively supports housing and urban redevelopment initiatives within its community development division. Every year, the bank invests billions of dollars in affordable and workforce housing through construction lending, investments in LIHTCs, and investments in mission-based real estate funds and individual development projects.

The bank also operates a real estate development arm, the Banc of America Community Development Corporation (BACDC), that works in partnership with public sector agencies, community-based nonprofit organizations, and for-profit developers to produce affordable and workforce housing while stimulating community revitalization. The projects in its Workforce Housing Development program are typically new or rehabilitated multifamily developments, and sometimes mixed-use projects, located in low- or moderate-income communities in markets where the bank has a strong presence. Most of the multifamily developments are mixed income and serve residents earning 50 to 100 percent of the AMI.[14]

Among many for-profit developers, Corcoran Jennison Companies has been a pioneer in building and managing mixed-income developments since 1971. Today, Corcoran Jennison owns and manages about 25,000 units in mixed-income properties in 12 states. One of the firm's specialties is redeveloping distressed public and other urban housing into mixed-income communities, including a number of HOPE VI projects.

McCormack Baron Salazar (MBS) is a St. Louis–based for-profit firm that specializes in the redevelopment of disinvested urban communities into thriving, economically integrated neighborhoods. Since 1973, MBS has developed more than 11,500 units of affordable and market-rate housing in 100 developments in 25 cities across the United States, including Kansas City, Cleveland, Pittsburgh, Los Angeles, San Francisco, Phoenix, Fort Worth, Atlanta, Richmond (Virginia), Minneapolis, Highland Park (Michigan), New Haven (Connecticut), and New York City. Most of the projects are rentals, although the firm has incorporated some for-sale housing in its developments. MBS manages all of its rental properties as well as 5,000 other properties nationwide.

The success of MBS's developments hinges on mixing incomes: in most of the firm's projects, between 50 and 60 percent of the units are reserved for low- and moderate-income families. The firm takes great care to ensure that the units appeal to those paying full rents.

Some market-rate development companies are adding affordable housing to their mix as a way to give something back but also to diversify and expand their markets. Often working with government agencies and/or nonprofit organizations, developers are overcoming the many obstacles to produce affordable housing. For example, affordable housing has been built into the mix at Stapleton, in Denver, where Forest City, the developer, established a comprehensive affordable housing program that includes working with local nonprofit housing agencies and builders to build affordable housing. Forest City provides technical expertise and guidance to the developers. The Stapleton affordable housing program specifies that

the affordable units must be developed in mixed-income neighborhoods and must adhere to minimum square footage guidelines. Ten percent of the single-family homes sold will be built under the HomeBuyer Resource Program, designed to put housing within reach of teachers, nurses, police officers, and other members of the community's workforce.

Ironically, the majority of Americans benefit from the very trends that cause the country's affordable housing crisis. With close to 70 percent of American households owning their own home, rapidly escalating home prices translate to increased equity, thus increased wealth and disposable income for many homeowners. In most cities, housing appreciation has outpaced gains in income, so not only has housing affordability declined but also the gap between the financial situation of homeowners and nonhomeowners has widened. Millions of housing "have-nots" have seen the dream of homeownership slip farther from view while their relative financial situation deteriorates. Public, private, and nonprofit organizations must come together to find ways to help the increasing numbers of under-housed and homeless families who are mere spectators rather than participants in the American dream.

Notes

[1] *The State of the Nation's Housing, 2004* (Cambridge, Massachusetts: Joint Center for Housing Studies of Harvard University, 2004).

[2] *Ibid.*

[3] *Ibid.*

[4] Millennial Housing Commission, *Meeting Our Nation's Housing Challenges* (Washington, D.C.: U.S. Government Printing Office, 2002).

[5] *The State of the Nation's Housing, 2004.*

[6] Bonnie Heudorfer, Barry Bluestone, and Stein Helmrich, *The Greater Boston Housing Report Card, 2003* (Boston, Massachusetts: Center for Urban and Regional Policy, Northeastern University, 2004).

[7] www.phfa.org.

[8] www.housingtrustfund.org.

[9] www.nrha.norfolk.va.us.

[10] www.nlihc.org.

[11] www.housingpartnership.net.

[12] www.lisc.org.

[13] www.gmhf.com.

[14] www.bankofamerica.com.

Affordable housing has become an important niche in the practice of architecture. Many architects have made affordable housing their major focus and are designing extraordinary projects. Some developers of this type of housing have become patrons of architecture, producing handsome developments that are also workable for their management companies. In fact, the design of affordable housing often is better than the architecture of market-rate production housing.

The reasons are multiple. Sometimes a limited budget can force greater creativity. Although high-end housing can use square footage as its marketing tool, affordable housing must rely on design and efficient use of space and materials. And although higher-priced housing must only please its buyer, an affordable community must appeal to the surrounding community as a way to overcome its objections. Good design is absolutely essential for the long-term good of affordable housing. The more that people are proud of where they live, the greater the likelihood that they will work harder to take care of their homes. And the better the housing looks, the greater the likelihood that neighborhoods will accept it in their backyards. Design must be used as a tool to change the public's often negative opinion toward introducing affordable housing into their neighborhoods.

In many cases, a proposal for a low-income project is initially rejected by its neighbors. But with an inclusive approach to planning, and a design that fits the surroundings, the community ultimately embraces the new development and even considers it an asset. Pyatok Architects, Inc., designed a 50-unit project on one acre in Palo Alto, California, an upper-middle-class university town. The project abuts a neighborhood of attractive single-family houses, both large and small. Adding such a dense development to this kind of community would naturally cause concern among neighbors. But the design solution reflects the surrounding neighborhood's scale and character. Instead of a continuous streetwall, which would have appeared out of context with the neighborhood, the project was designed so that the housing wraps around a series of U-shaped courtyards, creating a rhythm from the street of house, courtyard, house, courtyard. The house at the street edge is really the front for four or five houses in a row behind it, but on the street the view is similar to that of the surrounding single-family neighborhood. With compatible rooflines, porches, bay windows, and classic facades, the project gained the support of the neighborhood. And despite its architectural excellence, it was no more costly than if it had not been expertly designed.

COSTS AND AFFORDABILITY

Architects, planners, and housing designers cannot help but dream about some technical solutions to the worsening affordability problem. Higher densities could lower soft costs and land costs per unit, or prefabricated elements could speed the building process while relying on more cost-effective factory labor. Smaller, more efficient dwellings can save materials, and better insulation and orientation help to conserve energy. But in a booming economy with labor shortages and runaway land speculation, even major construction breakthroughs and technical design innovations have only limited ability to lower development costs. Further, major technical innovations always face problems of acceptance among labor, suppliers, and consumers, so benefits from such innovations are quickly minimized. And soft costs (interest, fees, profit margins) represent a significant portion of the cost of development over which there is little control. Even if innovations in methods or materials could lower production costs by as much as 10 percent, it may represent only a 5 percent reduction in sale prices. And just a half percent jump in the mortgage interest rate would wipe out that savings.

Another way to approach affordability is from consumers' point of view. If housing designers recognize that the difficulty of keeping housing costs affordable has more to do with household income than housing costs, perhaps they can better plan communities to allow for more income-generating opportunities. By allowing more creative and flexible live/work situations, households can have appropriate space for entrepreneurial activities that can boost their incomes.

INAPPROPRIATE REGULATION

Sometimes architects and planners can do more harm than good. Too often architects and designers believe that the needs of lower-income communities should be met with the same types of housing as middle-income communities. For example, 20th-century single-use zoning, which created isolated residential neighborhoods devoid of services or employment, has systematically made life more difficult for lower-income households. Typically, these neighborhoods lack transportation options and they prohibit using homes as income-producing workshops, stores, or sites for other forms of entrepreneurial activity that do not fit the tidy model of domestic retreat.

Inclusionary zoning, which encourages mixed-income neighborhoods, is often seen as a way to provide more affordable housing without creating islands of poverty. It has a place in some circumstances but is actually harmful in others. For example, when applied to communities with a long tradition of racially and culturally cohesive lower-income neighborhoods with their own community-based development corporation, inclusionary zoning can be very inappropriate. Further, private developers taking a cookie-cutter approach to developing mixed-income or affordable housing can overlook the potential for allowing community-based self-help organizations to learn how to solve the same problems themselves, learning to better serve their needs and gaining valuable skills along the way.

Finally, income limits that may accompany some forms of subsidized housing can have a significant dampening effect on home-grown entrepreneurial efforts. Contradictory government policies that, on the one hand, seek to encourage economic self-help activities but then, on the other, prematurely withdraw housing support at the first sign of success need to be reexamined, perhaps offering more gradual reductions in housing assistance as income improves.

Several communities have developed approaches to low-income housing that empower residents, override conventional rules, and build what best suits their needs. The following paragraphs describe three such examples.

Southern California

A Latino neighborhood sued a predominantly white upper-middle-class city in southern California for not producing its fair share of affordable housing. In response, the city offered inclusionary housing. But the Latinos refused. They wanted to live in a cohesive community where they could maintain their cultural traditions. They also wanted the political clout they could have only by remaining geographically cohesive. Finally, they wanted to form their own development corporation to build their own housing, increasing their own economic capacity and development skills. In short, they wanted to determine their own destinies—something that would be impossible if outside developers did it all for them and installed them as a 20 percent minority presence in someone else's culture and economy. Less than three years after the lawsuit, the community had developed a mixed-use housing development of nearly 100 units, followed by hundreds more affordable housing units, a teen recreation center, a child care center, and more. None of these uses would have been possible in an inclusionary model.

Seattle, Washington

A nonprofit corporation organized four different language groups of southeast Asian immigrants to get affordable housing to meet their needs. Offered an inclusionary opportunity in a suburban subdivision, they agreed on one condition: they would coexist with the predominantly white suburb only if their housing were developed by a nonprofit organization that serves the needs of Asian immigrants and not by the developer of the rest of the subdivision. They had several reasons: 1) the codes, covenants, and restrictions that accompanied the larger subdivision prohibited many activities that typify their cultures: laundry drying outdoors, food hanging from porches to dry in the sun, large community vegetable gardens in public view, religious rituals in open public spaces, combining houses for large family clans; 2) they wanted the architectural character to reflect their cultural traditions; and 3) they wanted their nonprofit to gain expertise in developing this type of housing.

The immigrant community has since developed a 53-unit affordable housing project with a 6,000-square-foot vegetable garden and community pig-roasting area, and front and back porches designed for hanging clothes and drying foods. The development is designed so that these activities do not face the surrounding subdivision; the surrounding community exerted control only over the colors of the buildings.

Oakland, California

A coalition of homeless citizens in downtown Oakland staged a series of sit-ins to protest office development that had claimed a formerly residential neighborhood. After much embarrassing publicity, the city council gave the organization $1 million to purchase land to build affordable housing. After a series of participatory design workshops, the coalition designed a 26-unit project with a child care center on a site of about one-third of an acre. With money from an arts foundation, the building was decorated with tiles designed by an African American artist inspired by the colors, patterns, and symbols of west African houses. The building is also graced with three "spirit houses" to provide homes for the earth spirits that the Buddhist community believes live on a property before a building is built.

As shown in these examples, design professionals can work with community groups to implement zoning changes and grant variances in much the same way that higher-income communities manipulate these laws. They can also work with groups to promote alternative development strategies. With strong community support and participation, a single project can be the catalyst for altering citywide zoning regulations and planning guidelines that consciously or unconsciously prevent affordable, socially controlled housing or more compact, efficient plans.

PUBLIC PARTICIPATION IN THE DESIGN PROCESS

Community design is an intense cultural enterprise that should be transparent and inclusive. The best architects and planners embrace this notion, working within a process that encourages hands-on public participation in the actual design of projects. Such team efforts welcome all stakeholders to the table. Community representatives are brought into the design process at the early stages, when they can be a part of the decision making, rather than being invited to the often unproductive and contentious public hearings held after the design has been established.

From the beginning of the design process, all parties must engage in a mutual educational process involving those who hold the long view of environmental and cultural impacts, those who hold the local, sometimes self-serving view, and those with the shortest view seeking immediate profits from a real estate deal. Designers can be the facilitators in the process. Sometimes called a "charrette" or a "participatory design workshop," this kind of interactive process enables the development team to reach a consensus and be able to move forward without the usual hostility. The process typically involves a series of workshops and meetings, with the result usually a concept plan from which the design team works to refine the plan and work out the details.

Although speed and efficiency are critical to housing production, avoiding the collective design process will only delay production in the long run. The cumulative resistance to change by communities confronting developers will only feed their belief that they are victims. It becomes an immutable force against all growth, without regard to quality or benefit. Recognizing that local populations need to be treated as partners in development at the very beginning of design, developers—for-profit, nonprofit, and public alike—will in the long run improve the climate for achieving higher-density, more compact mixed-use and mixed-income communities.

LIVE/WORK ENVIRONMENTS AS A WAY TO INCREASE AFFORDABILITY

Households at the lower economic rungs face similar necessities for survival as their American forebears who were colonists, pioneers, or immigrants. They share a clear pattern of strategies for coping with their financial limitations. First and foremost, they stay close to their source of livelihood to minimize their transportation costs, living adjacent to the fields, factories, or businesses where they work. Planning more mixed-use neighborhoods offering a wide variety of work opportunities along with good public transit may be the single most important contribution to housing affordability.

Households with limited incomes demonstrate another time-tested strategy for lowering the costs of living: earning income by working at home. But today's underclass faces additional obstacles to their survival not experienced by those in the past: zoning and building codes, insurance and lending practices, and property management attitudes that, while ostensibly protecting the health and safety of everyone, too often stifle the entrepreneurial needs of struggling families in the lower economic strata.

Obvious contemporary examples of live/work arrangements are computer-based activities. But not so obvious to white-collar housing policy makers are those who earn their additional incomes by repairing appliances, making clothing, running catering businesses, manufacturing and assembling toys, or providing all manner of services from hair and nail salons to body-building personal training, all undertaken in the confines of home.

A more creative approach needs to be taken toward mixing housing and workplace, without compromising the community's health and safety. For example, alley-served neighborhoods offer opportunities for messy private rear lots with manicured public fronts. If special fire separations were introduced between front and back portions of alley-served housing, the back half of a home could even be used for semi-industrial work.

Accommodating work in the home does not necessarily mean enlarging the housing. Instead, designers can look to what immigrants, pioneers, colonists, and low-income people around the world do. They shrink the living portion of the house to its basic essentials, releasing space for their income-producing activity. For example, a 1,100-square-foot, three-bedroom unit can easily occupy only 900 square feet of living space, freeing up the remaining 200 square feet for work. That space should be accessible directly from the outside, so it can function as a business independent of living space. Alternatively, a door to the work space can be located immediately off the foyer so that business activity does not invade the privacy of the living space. If the residents choose not to use the space for a business, it can become living space that can be rented for additional income or more space for the family.

For example, Hismen Hin-Nu Terrace in Oakland, California, is located on a major boulevard that formerly hosted several miles of neighborhood retail shops before the construction of a nearby parallel freeway. The project consists of residential units on upper floors with a market hall on the main level for small startup craft and clothing vendors. Along the outside edge of the market hall is a row of indented niches for street vendors' incubator businesses. Designed independently of the housing, the space is available for residents of the complex to begin their own businesses.

Also in Oakland is International Boulevard Housing, a development that includes ground-floor units zoned and designed to allow occupants to produce goods or services. Each unit has a front room with storefront windows, four-plex electrical outlets at the bottom and tops of walls, a large stainless steel work sink in the lavatory, and double pocket doors so that the business can be expanded to the rear of the unit or closed off to keep the rear private. Each unit has a blade sign and metal canopy at the front street entry to announce the business. The spandrel zone above the storefront windows is designed to receive artwork depicting the purpose of the business below. These ground-floor units can be serviced from the parking court to the rear.

In Tacoma, Washington, Martin Luther King Homes is located on a former retail street whose zoning still permits nonresidential uses. These homes for first-time buyers have two front entrances, one from a rear court for the family and one into a front room facing the street for guests or possible business customers. This room has extra volume and can be segregated from the rest of the house if the household chooses to use it as a business.

Sycamore Street Co-op, a rental housing development in Santa Cruz, California, is located on a former industrial site. Funded with tax credits, the residences are three-story townhouses with a bedroom and full bath on the ground floor that can be sublet to renters or used for a small home-based business accessed from an entry foyer. The kitchen, dining area, and living space are on the second level, while two more bedrooms and a bath are on the third level.

These examples demonstrate just a few ways to use a home to create additional sources of income. In terms of planning, every situation is different. In some cases, permissive zoning is already in place, but others may require variances or a change in zoning to permit mixed uses. Increased parking requirements to accommodate potential customers or accessory units may be needed. Or relief from these requirements may be granted.

Residents are the obvious beneficiaries of creative housing solutions. But others benefit as well: more stable and improving incomes means lenders see a reduction in mortgage defaults, landlords see a reduction in missed rent payments, local businesses see increased activity from the expanded buying power of residents, and neighborhoods become more stable. And all of these outcomes are accomplished without the need for magical technological breakthroughs.

Since the 1950s, urban public housing projects have clearly demonstrated that isolating and warehousing low-income families is a formula for social disaster. It is also inconsistent with the American concept of assimilating diverse ethnic groups and the economically disadvantaged into the mainstream of American life. In recent years, for-profit developers have been a driving force in breaking down old models and creating a new generation of housing that blends affordable units into a mixed-income setting.

What attracts these developers to affordable housing? There's no question that they are in the business for the same reason as other developers: to make a profit. But there are other reasons as well. Developers of affordable housing see their business as an opportunity to reinvest in cities and to meet the housing needs for working families and low-income households.

Corcoran Jennison Companies is a pioneer in developing mixed-income housing. Joseph E. Corcoran, the company's chair, grew up in the Dorchester neighborhood of Boston, where professors and doctors lived side by side with laborers and small businessmen, the unemployed, and the inebriated. Corcoran, the youngest son of Irish immigrants, witnessed firsthand that people of different incomes and races could live together. "When we started developing this type of housing in 1971, everyone said we would fail, that it would never work. But I knew it would work, because I grew up in a neighborhood that was textbook American melting pot, a great community where all ethnic groups got along."

Richard Baron of McCormack Baron Salazar, Inc., based in St. Louis, focuses on blighted neighborhoods that have lost their market value to reclaim those areas and provide a quality living environment. Baron's interest in this type of housing began when he worked as a legal services attorney just out of law school. At that time, he and his partner, the late Terry McCormack, saw an opportunity in blighted neighborhoods to create better communities and to still make a living. "This type of housing is not as lucrative for us as other types of housing could be. But we are able to do well and do good in this business, and in the process we have served thousands of families and children, working with schools, and training and creating jobs for residents."

A NEW IMAGE FOR AFFORDABLE HOUSING

According to the National Association of Counties, nearly 85 percent of new housing in the United States is targeted to middle- and upper-income households, not working families. One of the major reasons is that community resistance has been so successful at preventing the construction of new affordable housing. Imagining the worst, NIMBY (not in my backyard) factions believe that affordable housing will cause neighborhood blight and decline. But developers like Corcoran Jennison and McCormack Baron Salazar are working to defeat old stereotypes.

To begin, they seldom use the word "affordable." Not only does it scare off the neighbors, it creates a self-esteem issue for residents and a public relations issue for developers. Instead, they term their developments "mixed-income communities," a term that more closely defines most of the communities they build. They are, in fact, communities where residents paying market rents (the highest rents the project can achieve in that area) live side by side with residents who qualify for some kind of housing assistance. Corcoran Jennison does manage a number of communities in which all units are subsidized, but even in those properties "affordable" is a word to be avoided because of negative connotations in the marketplace.

In multifamily projects, rents are based on many criteria, including project costs and market demands for the area. To attract residents to any kind of residential project, subsidized or not, the property must be impeccably maintained and look better than the competition, whether it is a high-end luxury complex or a project receiving tax credits. The key to success for affordable housing is to offer attractive design and amenities and to treat all residents the same, whether their monthly rent is $500 or $2,500.

PUTTING THE PIECES TOGETHER: LAYERS OF FINANCING

In 1974, Massachusetts was the first state in the country to create a state housing finance agency (HFA), but soon other states across the country followed. State HFAs offered multifamily developers low-interest loans in return for the owners' agreeing to include a certain percentage of affordable units. During the Reagan Administration (1980–1988), federal housing subsidy programs were reduced to an all-time low, and production of new low-income housing was virtually stopped. Small nonprofit housing providers tried to pick up the slack with very-small-scale projects, relying on grassroots financing from foundations or capitalizing on bank foreclosures.

In the 1990s, for-profit multifamily developers were back in the game, with HUD initiatives like the HOPE VI program transforming public housing into private developments. Nonprofit housing developers grew in size to resemble their for-profit counterparts. But federal programs come and go, so financing affordable housing is a moving target. Programs and requirements change, and developers are constantly adjusting their financing packages. It is not unusual for a developer to have to coordinate as many as six or seven sources of financing to make just one affordable housing project happen.

Currently, the government subsidy for all low-income and affordable housing initiatives represents $50 billion a year. By comparison, the 2004 subsidy to homeowners in the form of federal tax deductions for property taxes, mortgage interest, and exclusion of capital gains is estimated at $107 billion,[1] or more than twice that amount. Yet government-assisted financing for programs that would help stimulate production of affordable housing continues to be reduced. If necessity is the mother of invention, the positive outcome of this situation is that, as the federal government backs away, state and local agencies have become more creative in coming up with alternative programs.

HOPE VI has been a success in targeting and redeveloping the worst public housing, but Richard Baron believes a program needs to be created that provides options for communities to develop housing and allow for other uses as well, including schools and retail shops. Such a program would look more like the old urban development action grants from HUD. The key, Baron says, is flexibility. Funds would go to the areas in the communities with the most needs, and those communities could decide whether housing alone or housing combined with other uses would better serve them.

"Real changes in a community take place with an integrated plan that targets many areas—not just the housing we build but the total community where the housing is," says Baron. "To help us change entire communities, not just the housing, we need programs that don't come with strings and bureaucracy."

PROPERTY MANAGEMENT: A KEY ELEMENT

Good design, while crucial for a successful development, will not in itself solve social or economic problems. For a project to be successful, its developers must have a sense of stewardship for the entire community. They must be prepared to take on responsibilities for the social issues of the communities they build. Providing management expertise with an understanding of residents' needs is an important part of managing affordable communities. To do so, they must include residents' participation in a way that is productive for both the residents and the property. And property management cannot be successful without resident services.

Resident Participation:
Empowerment versus Management

Most of the nation's largest institutional investors and property owners do not manage their own properties because they do not have the required skills. The same is true for tenant and resident organizations. In four of its public housing turnarounds, Corcoran Jennison has established a legal joint venture with an elected resident group. As empowered owners, resident organizations act jointly with the developers to direct management to perform to certain standards. The development firm retains the right to dismiss the management company if it is not doing its job. This kind of management arrangement offers true empowerment for residents without having the complex day-to-day burdens of property management.

Resident Services

Resident services are an important part of the management package in today's affordable housing world, but they were not always. In the 1970s, resident services were unheard of. Yet the need for social services that would work with the ownership was crucial in communities with significant social problems or where major rehabilitation was about to occur. For their first affordable housing project, Corcoran Jennison hired Housing Opportunities, a newly formed private social service agency. If a resident had a problem paying rent, resident services would work with management to devise a payment plan and with the resident to make sure he or she adhered to it. If a drug or alcohol problem surfaced, resident services became involved to find treatment. Relying on the resident services team allows the owner/developer/manager to concentrate on the business of real estate, while the resident service provider concentrates on the social issues that need attention in the community.

Over the years, Corcoran Jennison has learned that resident services are helpful not only in severely distressed turnaround properties but also on a smaller scale at other sites. Resident services can tackle needs that management cannot and is not trained to provide: after-school programs for latch-key children, job training and résumé building, basic financial planning education to further residents' self-reliance, for example.

Other development firms have created models of resident services that work. The partnership that developed Belle Creek, a mixed-income community in Denver, for example, included Rocky Mountain Mutual Housing, a nonprofit with a solid track record in low- and moderate-income housing to manage the rental apartment component of the community. Mutual provides residents with the tools they need to become self-sufficient, including financial management education, job training, daycare, and equity building to facilitate homeownership. Residents make up more than half of the board of directors and are involved in management decisions.

Resident services providers gain support from the community by offering the services that are most in demand. If programming offered is dictated by the property owner or manager or by government agencies, the programming is doomed. One resident services provider, Housing Opportunities Unlimited, begins by surveying residents to identify the needs of the community and then delivers programs based on surveys. The dollars spent on resident services are carefully targeted to areas where participation is guaranteed. Residents will respond only to a program they have designed themselves.

Other developers share this view of resident services. McCormack Baron Salazar extends its reach beyond its property line. As part of the firm's development strategy, it first determines what factors of the community at large will positively or negatively affect the project and then determines how to address or improve those situations. It sees schools as a good place to begin. In St. Louis, McCormack Baron Salazar has a project located near Jefferson Elementary School, in a census tract with the lowest median income in the city. McCormack Baron Salazar helped raise $3.5 million to make physical and other improvements geared to changing students' performance at the school. Through a new and accelerated visual arts program, the school mandates that parents become involved in their children's education. The program has been successful at involving parents and students in the programming. More important than the money, says Richard Baron, is the collaboration with the business community, which became an integrated part of the effort to change the community.

Often, affordable communities do not generate additional cash for resident services and so must solicit funding from federal and private grants so that they can make these services available to residents. One federal program is Neighborhood Network Centers (NNC), a HUD initiative in which funds for on-site computer centers are as much as 100 percent generated philanthropically from local businesses. Goals are to improve computer access and literacy, to prepare residents for employment opportunities, and to provide access to information on health care and social services. A computer room is designated at the NNC, and local vendors and merchants donate time and equipment. Schools supply volunteers to teach residents computer skills. More than 1,100 NNCs currently exist, providing resources for residents.

Developers like Corcoran Jennison and McCormack Baron Salazar agree that extra dollars spent on resident services help build strong communities. From the perspective of operation, on-site services and working with the community beyond the development's borders help to eliminate vandalism, reduce rent arrearages, and increase residents' satisfaction.

Richard Baron likes to say "do well and do good," and his goal has always been to build a better way of life for families and their children in the inner city. Joe Corcoran's determination to keep creating successful mixed-income neighborhoods is a result of his growing up in one. Both agree that developing successful affordable housing can happen only when we leave behind the word "affordable" and start thinking about quality mixed-income communities—socially vibrant, financially solvent, and well designed—that everyone and anyone would be proud to call home.

Note

1. Joint Committee on Taxation, *Estimates of Federal Tax Expenditures for Fiscal Years 2002–2006* (Washington, D.C.: U.S. Government Printing Office, January 17, 2002), Table 1.

CASE STUDIES

Across the country, communities, nonprofit organizations, and developers are finding small-scale affordable housing solutions that provide high-quality homes for a fortunate few. Although these solutions are not able to provide housing for all who need it, they do offer hope and serve as examples of what can be accomplished.

Such community-based local projects show that multiple approaches are needed to address this housing crisis. Each of the following examples has taken into account the distinctive histories, contexts, sites, and populations of the communities and neighborhoods where they are located. In the past, many housing projects did not address such crucial factors. A one-size-fits-all approach was common as communities displaced in the name of slum clearance or urban renewal were relocated in overwhelming towers or barracks-style housing projects. These past approaches are why housing projects of previous eras, from New York to Los Angeles, can look strikingly similar—and decidedly unattractive.

Many of today's affordable housing projects are indistinguishable from their market-rate neighbors. By taking into account their surroundings, affordable housing projects have assumed myriad building types and forms: from single-family homes to high-rise multi-family buildings. The change in how affordable housing is being designed and built is one of the motivating factors behind the National Building Museum's exhibition *Affordable Housing: Designing an American Asset*. It demonstrates the diversity and vibrancy of the different approaches to affordable housing.

In choosing the 18 examples presented in the exhibit and in this companion piece, the museum's curators sought projects from every region of the nation to represent the diverse building types and architectural styles found in affordable housing projects. Among the examples are mixed-use developments, mixed-income communities, adaptive use projects, and rehabilitation/historic preservation. The curators also wanted to show the range of people who need affordable housing. Represented among the 18 case studies are projects for families with small children, single adults, the elderly, farmworkers, the developmentally disabled, the formerly homeless, and more.

In addition to demonstrating the diversity and range of what has been built, the curators used the exhibition to show that affordable housing can meet high standards of design. They used five criteria to guide them:

1. *Are the grounds clearly marked in such a way as to indicate ownership and use?* Such indicators include walkways, curbs, fences, walls, and hedges. Delineating ownership in this manner has been shown to reduce crime, increase residents' feelings of security, and generate pride in one's home, which translates to improved maintenance.

2. *Does a sequence or continuum help the transition from public space to private space?* Porches, entrances, lobbies, foyers, and hallways are all examples of how transitional spaces can move one from public spaces (such as parks, sidewalks, and streets) to private spaces (such as the inside of one's home or backyard). Public views of private spaces should be minimized and shielded. When designed well, these transitional spaces can foster a welcoming feeling of friendliness while still preserving residents' privacy.

3. *Do the different sides of the buildings help create and define how the different spaces are used?* The different sides of a building can create opportunities for distinctions between public and private, tidy and untidy, ceremonial and service spaces. The urban rowhouse, for example, defines the streetscape while providing privacy and service areas in the rear.

Building Types Found in Case Studies

	Single-Family Detached Houses	Single-Family Attached Houses	Low-Rise Multifamily Buildings	Mid-Rise Multifamily Buildings	Group Residences
11th Avenue Townhomes		●			
101 San Fernando				●	
Archer Courts			●	●	
Auburn Court			●		
Chelsea Court				●	●
College Park	●				
Colorado Court				●	
Dove Street			●		●
Howard/LeDroit		●			
La Cascada II			●		
Mozingo Place			●		
Row 8.9n		●		●	
Stoney Pine			●		
Swan's Market			●		
Tierra Nueva		●			
Townhomes on Capitol Hill		●			
Waterloo Heights			●		●
Westbury	●				

4. *How do the units differ in relation to their location in the project?* The conditions of each unit do not need to be identical but rather should reflect the particular benefits of each unit's location. For example, the end townhouse should have a different plan from the interior units. Such compensating amenities can make units distinctive and stands in opposition to the rigid conformity of units and buildings found in many residential developments (both affordable and market rate).

5. *How flexible is the layout of the units and of the project as a whole?* Flexibility in design can allow for different household types, different furnishings, easy expansion, reinterpretation of space, and personalization by residents. Flexibility in design should create opportunities for residents to simply and unobtrusively make their dwellings their own.

In her 1961 rallying cry for urbanism, *The Death and Life of Great American Cities,* author Jane Jacobs describes in great detail the importance of mixed-use neighborhoods. Since then, people have started to appreciate existing mixed-use buildings and have created many more such communities and neighborhoods. Mixing various land uses can provide a critical mass and a sense of place that establishes a strong identity. In a mixed-use environment, the range of uses can add value and economic vitality to a community. When affordable housing is included in a mixed-use neighborhood, the residents benefit from their proximity to the other uses and save money on transportation. Residents in mixed-use communities may also have more opportunities to live and work in the same area, thus further cutting down on transportation costs.

The idea of mixing incomes in residential settings is not new: urban neighborhoods traditionally have contained a mix of housing products suitable for an array of incomes. More recently, mixing incomes has become a way to supply affordable housing options, increase absorption in large planned developments, revitalize urban neighborhoods, and decrease the concentration of poverty in publicly assisted housing.

In many cases, mixed-income housing projects are even part of economic development packages to revitalize neighborhoods.

Rehabilitating aging structures helps preserve our nation's architectural heritage, and the adaptive use or rehabilitation of existing structures is becoming more common in affordable housing projects. The adaptive use of old buildings offers character and charm as well as the chance to preserve a historically important streetscape or building facade.

Vulnerable and special-needs populations are disproportionately affected by shortages in housing. On top of the normal challenges faced by those who want to build affordable housing, those who develop special-needs housing can face even tougher obstacles. The inclusion of projects for such populations in the exhibition represents the developers' triumphs over a wide range of challenges—from the surrounding communities' rejection or acceptance of a project to the challenges inherent in housing a special-needs population. For example, Mozingo Place offers on-site psychological counseling for some of its residents, Tierra Nueva includes a Head Start office for the children of migrant farm workers, and Dove Street Independent Housing includes ample storage space so that the people living with AIDS can store their various medicines and medical equipment inconspicuously.

The 18 projects presented in the exhibition and in this accompanying publication represent some of the best practices in affordable housing today. Although the future of many effective housing programs such as HUD's HOPE VI and Section 8 programs is in question, it seems that communities everywhere are starting to realize the impact affordable housing can have in improving the quality of life for all citizens—both for those who need housing and for those who share their neighborhoods.

Development Strategies and Characteristics of the Case Study Projects

	Neighborhood Revitalization	Mixed Uses	Mixed Incomes	Special Needs/ Disability	Rehab/Reuse
11th Avenue Townhomes	✓				
101 San Fernando	✓	✓	✓		
Archer Courts	✓		✓		✓
Auburn Court	✓		✓		
Chelsea Court	✓			✓	✓
College Park			✓		
Colorado Court					
Dove Street				✓	
Howard/LeDroit	✓		✓		✓
La Cascada II	✓			✓	
Mozingo Place	✓	✓		✓	✓
Row 8.9n	✓		✓		
Stoney Pine			✓	✓	
Swan's Market	✓	✓	✓		✓
Tierra Nueva					
Townhomes on Capitol Hill	✓		✓		
Waterloo Heights				✓	
Westbury	✓		✓		

Neighborhood Revitalization:
Is the project specifically designed to encourage neighborhood regeneration?

Mixed Uses:
Does the project include a mix of uses besides housing?

Mixed Incomes:
Is the project intended to create a mixed-income community?

Special Needs/Disability:
Is the housing designed for people living with disabilities or infirmities who have certain needs, such as wheelchair-bound individuals, people living with AIDS, people with developmental problems, for example?

Rehab/Reuse:
Did developers choose to renovate an existing structure rather than building from scratch?

Escondido, California, is a city of about 150,000 people located 30 miles to the northeast of San Diego. Although its market-rate housing is more affordable than that of most communities in San Diego County— according to the city's official Web site, Escondido has the lowest median housing prices in the county—even there more affordable housing is needed.

To meet this need, SER Incorporated, a local nonprofit organization devoted to education, job skills training, literacy, employment opportunities, and accessing affordable housing in the San Diego area, developed 11th Avenue Townhomes.

The project was funded largely through low-income housing tax credits, with additional funding in the form of community development block grants and HOME grants. At only 16 units, the project was initially over-looked in the LIHTC application process. It was on its third application attempt that investors began to appreciate the financial feasibility of the project.

Originally part of a large citrus ranch, the properties adjacent to the site recall the region's history. An avocado and citrus fruit orchard from the 1880s, a remnant of the area's agricultural past, is very close to the development. Bungalow cottages built between 1900 and the 1940s border one side of 11th Avenue Townhomes. Nearby, an early motor court motel from the 1940s marks the beginnings of southern California's car culture. Also adjacent to the project is a trailer park that was established in the 1970s.

The deep and narrow parcel guided many of the project's design considerations. As a result, the development features two rows of attached townhouses fronting a narrow, tree-lined lane. Both pedestrians and automobiles share access to this central passageway. The arrangement of the compact structures is reminiscent of southern California's bungalow courts and London mews. The project also includes a tot lot, a vegetable garden, and

a meeting hall for residents' gatherings and other activities. The meeting hall sits across from a shady plaza and open lawn.

Given that an estimated 42 percent of Escondido residents are Latino, Studio E, the architecture firm, designed the project with the Latino community in mind. While taking into account cultural considerations, Studio E also had to maximize space creatively on an awkwardly shaped parcel.

Based on Studio E's observation that Latino residents prefer to socialize in the frontyard rather than the back-yard, Studio E included a stoop and small frontyard for each unit that looks out onto the lane. The lane serves multiple functions, acting both as a driveway for all 16 of the units and as a social space. Speed bumps and other traffic calming features have made the lane a safe place for children to play and for adults to hang out and chat with their neighbors.

In addition to features intended to help with social interaction, carefully placed doors and windows in each unit help to facilitate child supervision as well as create cross ventilation. Layout and construction of the town-houses were kept simple. All of the units feature wood frame construction on a concrete foundation. Variations include two-, three-, and four-bedroom townhouses and three-bedroom flats. Circulation is minimized in the townhouses, and garden/patios at the rear extend the living area and offer private outdoor space. Depending on the renter's needs, the attached one-car garage could be adapted for use as an office, workshop, family room, or other use.

Area Median Income (family of 4)	$50,300
Residents Served	100% of units serve those at 40% of AMI

LAND USE INFORMATION

Site Area	0.85 acre
Total Dwelling Units	16
Gross Project Density	18.8 units per acre
Housing Type	Rental townhouses

RESIDENTIAL UNIT INFORMATION

Unit Type	Floor Area (Sq. Ft.)	No. Built	Rent (1st Month)
2-Bedroom/1-Bath	810	4	$550
3-Bedroom/2-Bath	1,040	8	$630
3-Bedroom/2-Bath	1,005	2	$630
4-Bedroom/2-Bath	1,295	2	$710

FUNDING SOURCES

Funding Source	Amount	% of Total
Equity from Federal Credit	$1,232,300	52
Western National Bank	173,300	7
AHP Western National Bank	39,600	2
City of Escondido CDBG	216,700	9
City of Escondido HOME	426,400	18
City of Escondido RDA	250,000	11
GP Equity	8,000	1
Total	$2,346,300	100

DEVELOPMENT COSTS

Development Cost Information	Amount	% of Total
Site Acquisition	$86,800	3.7
Site Improvement/Construction	1,224,800	52.8
Architectural Fees	137,800	5.9
Survey and Engineering	11,000	0.5
Construction Interest and Fees	126,200	5.4
Permanent Financing	6,000	0.3
Legal Fees	13,000	0.6
Reserves	32,000	1.4
Appraisal	6,000	0.3
Construction Contingencies	186,400	8.0
Developer's Costs	138,400	6.0
Other—Marketing, Furnishing, Inspections, Permit Processing Fees	351,800	15.2
Total	$2,320,200	100.0

©Brady

©Brady

DEVELOPMENT TEAM

Developer
SER Incorporated
San Diego, California

Architect
Studio E Architects
San Diego, California

Builder
Diversified Construction
San Diego, California

Landscape Architect
Katherine Stangle
San Diego, California

©Brady

In many ways, urban growth in Silicon Valley for the past 50 years has reflected national urban growth patterns and trends. Sometime in the 1950s, San Jose, at the center of Silicon Valley, went into a decline as people left cities in favor of nearby suburban enclaves. By the 1980s and 1990s, downtown San Jose was empty while surrounding suburban communities like Sunnyvale and Mountain View flourished. The superheated economy of the 1990s, the related skyrocketing real estate prices, and the traffic congestion enhanced by auto-dominant growth fueled a greater interest in urban alternatives to the undifferentiated suburban growth that had come to characterize the whole region south of San Francisco.

It was in this environment that the San Jose Redevelopment Agency (SJRA) was able to mobilize support and build momentum for growth in the downtown core. The high-density 101 San Fernando complex (107.7 dwelling units per acre) is part of a coordinated plan to bring life back to San Jose, taking its place among many regional draws in the downtown: the HP Pavilion, home of the San Jose Sharks hockey team, a brand new light-rail system, the impressive San Jose McEnery Convention Center, the Tech Museum, the Children's Discovery Museum of San Jose, the San Jose Museum of Art, many historic buildings, a new library, a symphony hall, and a new city hall and civic center complex designed by noted architect Richard Meier.

Despite many amenities in the downtown area and the lowest crime rate among cities its size, San Jose's downtown is still underused and is often bypassed for other more appealing communities. The role 101 San Fernando plays in the city's revitalization strategy is very important. Along with other acclaimed multifamily housing projects like the Colonnades, Paseo Plaza, and Santana Row, 101 San Fernando brings a 24-hour presence to downtown San Jose. Based on recommendations from a ULI Advisory Services report on the area in 2000, the city seeks more high-density residential and mixed-use buildings. Such buildings can bring much-needed housing and create a diverse range of new retail opportunities.

Even though San Jose has some of the lowest housing prices in Silicon Valley, housing costs still exclude many from homeownership. In 2000, the median price of a single-family home was $499,000, compared to $631,000 in Sunnyvale and $710,000 in Los Gatos. At the time 101 San Fernando was being planned, affordable housing was desperately needed everywhere in Silicon Valley.

Using tax increment financing, SJRA is devoted to bringing life back to downtown San Jose. Run by a board of directors comprising the mayor and city council members, SJRA works to foster downtown growth through investing in affordable housing, upgrading transportation options, preserving and rejuvenating buildings and neighborhoods, developing new cultural facilities, and encouraging private investment.

The 101 San Fernando site was originally used for a bank and its adjacent parking lot. Interested in developing the site, the landowner approached SJRA. SJRA and the landowner chose Forest City to develop the project, and the three organizations formed a partnership to build a mixed-income and mixed-use residential project on the site. SJRA bought the land, then leased it to Forest City. The seller of the land then contributed a portion of the land price to the partnership. As part of the agreement, SJRA paid for the costs associated with the temporary relocation of the bank. Upon completion of the project, the bank was returned to the site as one of the tenants in the building

Although 101 San Fernando was built with urbane young adults in mind, it has also become very appealing to empty nesters. The building's 322 rental units include studio and one-, two-, and three-bedroom floor plans. With 20 percent of the units serving those who earn less than 80 percent of the regional median income, the project is a combination of both market-rate and affordable housing.

Togawa & Smith, Architects, and Solomon E.T.C. Architecture and Urban Design worked together to create a balance between public and private space that characterizes the development and helps to foster social interaction and camaraderie among residents. The nearly three-acre site is organized around a series of mid-block pedestrian lanes. These passageways can be accessed through large gated portals in the street-front facade as well as from secured parking areas. The portals provide openness and multiple points of entry without sacrificing security. Lower-level units are accessible by stoops, while high-level units offer elevator access. The upper-level corridors feature outdoor loggias that offer views to the courtyards below. These features create multiple visual access points that help to encourage community interaction and create an increased feeling of safety by offering more eyes on the street. Thanks to this innovative design, 101 San Fernando won a 2003 AIA/HUD Housing and Design Award.

DEVELOPMENT TEAM

Developer
Forest City, L.A.
Los Angeles, California

Architects
Daniel F. Solomon
Solomon E.T.C., A WRT Company

Togawa & Smith, Architects
Pasadena, California

Landscape Architect
Guzzardo Associates
San Francisco, California

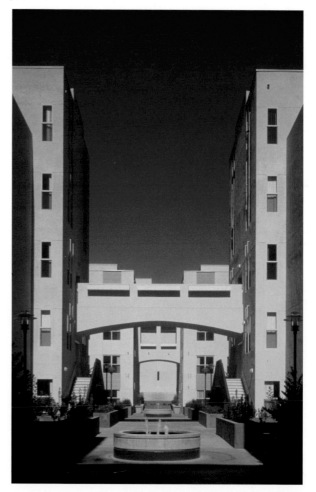

Russell Abraham, courtesy of Solomon E.T.C., a WRT Company

Area Median Income (family of 4)	$105,500
Residents Served	25% of units serve those at up to 80% of AMI

LAND USE INFORMATION

Site Area	2.99 acres
Total Dwelling Units	322
Gross Project Density	107.7 units per acre
Total Parking	564
Parking Ratio	1.75 cars per unit
Housing Type	Rental apartments

RESIDENTIAL UNIT INFORMATION

Unit Type

Market Rate	Floor Area (Sq. Ft.)	No. Built	Rent (1st Month)
Studio	537	27	$1,295
1-Bedroom	825	145	$1,495
2-Bedroom	1,326	81	$1,995
3-Bedroom	1,399	3	$3,353
Affordable			
Studio	537	7	$737
1-Bedroom	825	36	$782
2-Bedroom	1,326	23	$928
3-Bedroom	1,399	1	$1,070

DEVELOPMENT COSTS

Development Cost Information	Amount	% of Total
Land	$ 7,800,000	11
Direct Construction	49,074,600	66
Off-Site Costs	900,000	1
Architecture and Engineering	2,095,300	3
Permits and Fees	1,447,000	2
Marketing	724,200	1
Real Estate Taxes/Insurance/Legal	1,219,900	2
Developer's Overhead	1,518,900	2
Cost of Issuance	1,912,500	3
Other Financing Fees	2,349,700	3
Interest Reserve	1,449,100	2
Tenant Improvements	100,000	0
Tenant Relocation	650,000	1
Title and Closing	68,000	0
Contingencies	769,000	1
Total	**$72,078,200**	**100**

FUNDING SOURCES

Funding Source	Amount	% of Total
30-Year Variable Rate Demand Multifamily Housing Revenue Bonds	$38,000,000	55.1
Proceeds from Refinancing	3,000,000	4.4
City of San Jose Land Subsidy	7,000,000	10.2
Off-Site Subsidy	900,000	1.3
Subsidy for Relocation of Bank of America	1,200,000	1.8
Forest City and LIHTC Equity	17,897,800	25.9
Limited Partner Equity	1,000,000	1.4
Total	**$68,997,825**	**100.0**

The public housing projects of the Chicago Housing Authority (CHA) used to have a bad reputation. The towering high-rise buildings characteristic of Chicago's public housing have become symbols of modernist hubris and failed social policies. Based on unrealistic conceptions of how people live, these drab concrete buildings with chain link fenced corridors and steel windows did not instill pride in their residents. The high-rise buildings at Cabrini Green became a legendary tale of caution of what happens when the good intentions of public housing officials fail to deliver. Now roughly 50 years after being constructed, these buildings have weathered inadequate maintenance, race riots, drug wars, and unbelievable crime rates.

But CHA, the third largest public housing system in the nation, has a plan. The Chicago Housing Authority's Plan for Transformation is guiding the rehabilitation and demolition of more than 25,000 of its units. The goal is to create mixed-income communities comprising one-third public housing, one-third affordable housing, and one-third market-rate homes.

The redevelopment of Archer Courts now serves as a harbinger of hope for the projects that follow. Archer Courts is one of eight complexes ("Courts") to emerge from a city- and state-funded public housing program designed to house those displaced by the construction of the Eisenhower Expressway, a highway connecting the city to its western suburbs. Built in 1951, Archer Courts and its counterparts embodied the minimalist aesthetic of the modernists. Originally, Archer Courts consisted of two seven-story towers with a total of 147 units. One of the defining architectural features of these towers was the series of open-air corridors running the length of the buildings along the front facades. Chain link fences formed railings along these corridors.

Even before its rehabilitation, Archer Courts stood out from its counterparts. Although many of its counterparts became enveloped in terrible social issues, Archer Courts remained relatively safe, stable, and clean. Rather than tear down the buildings as recommended by both government officials and many neighborhood leaders, the Chicago Community Development Corporation saw in Archer Courts the chance to preserve a community comprising a unique mix of residents and a challenge to retrofit an aging utilitarian structure into a vibrant, safe, and attractive place.

Landon Bone Baker Architects incorporated input from community leaders and residents into its redesign and renovation of the complex. Feng Shui (a Chinese philosophy that the positioning of a building and all of its features can influence the lives of its residents) was employed in how the buildings and surrounding land were reconfigured. Primary elements of the interior rehabilitation include new elevators, mechanical systems, bathrooms, and kitchens. In addition, a wellness center is included for treatment of minor medical conditions, and a computer center offers classes and software in both English and Chinese. The landscaped grounds around the buildings provide a retreat from urban Chicago, with outdoor pavilions that provide space used for meditation and the practice of Tai Chi.

One of the biggest changes to the building was the enclosure of exposed corridors by a wall of glass. This glass "curtain wall" consists of many large panels of glass colored in a range of hues reflecting the colors of the interior doors. The result has dramatically changed aesthetic perceptions of the building from the inside and from afar. The front facade glistens in the sun, reflecting the light from the multicolored panels. Now that the corridors are shielded from the elements, their light and airy feeling has made them sites of informal socializing.

Phase II of Archer Courts saw the construction of 43 townhouses on the site's vacant land. Each two- and three-bedroom dwelling is designed with its own garage and roof deck. Walkways, landscaping, and architectural themes unify the two phases. Funding for Phase II came from the city of Chicago's Home Start program, an initiative that supports the development of slightly below-market-rate properties to encourage homeownership. Further, CHA will rent out four of these units as subsidized housing in return for contribution of the land.

To ensure affordability, the architect relied on a "kit of parts" for construction: a preengineered load-bearing, precast-concrete panel system, shop-fabricated steel window bays, aluminum windows, preengineered wood trusses, and precast concrete stairs. This process saved construction time and, in turn, labor costs. Furthermore, the city of Chicago is providing tax increment subsidies to write down the purchase price (to affordable levels) for five households with incomes at or below 80 percent of the area median income.

DEVELOPMENT TEAM

Developer
Chicago Community Development Corporation
Chicago, Illinois

Architect
Landon Bone Baker Architects
Chicago, Illinois

Builder
Burling Builders, Inc.
Chicago, Illinois

Landscape Architect
McKay Landscape Architects
Chicago, Illinois

Moy Got

Steinkamp/Ballogg Photography, Inc.

Area Median Income (family of 4)	$68,700
Residents Served	Phase I: 100% of units serve those at up to 50% of AMI. Phase II: 20% of units serve those at 80% of AMI

	Phase I	Phase II
Site Area	3.1 acres	1.1 acres
Total Dwelling Units	147	43
Gross Project Density	47.4 units per acre	41.4 units per acre
Housing Type	Apartments	Townhouses

	Phase I	Phase II
Number of Units Owned	0	39
Number of Units Rented	147	4

Unit Type	Floor Area (Sq. Ft.)	No. Built	Sale Price or Rent (1st Month)
Phase I			
1-Bedroom	467	106	$740
2-Bedroom	648	28	$888
3-Bedroom	790	13	$1,065
Phase II			
2-Bedroom*	1,800–1,850	23	$270,000
3-Bedroom*	1,840–2,270	20	$320,000
CHA Rental Housing— 2- and 3-Bedroom Units	1,800–2,270	4	**

* Five 2- and 3-bedroom units were reserved for those who earn less than 80 percent of the area median income. The average price for these affordable units was $150,000.

** 30% of adjusted gross income.

Funding Source	Amount	% of Total
Phase I		
City of Chicago Tax-Exempt Bonds	$4,541,800	39
City of Chicago CDBG	2,507,900	22
Chicago Housing Authority	650,000	6
Chicago Equity Fund LIHTCs	3,825,500	33
Total	**$11,525,200**	**100**
Phase II		
City of Chicago General Obligation Bonds	$2,061,500	15
City of Chicago HOMESTART Bond Proceeds	8,675,600	64
Portion of Proceeds from Unit Sales	1,649,400	12
Chicago Housing Authority Land Contribution	1,189,500	9
Total	**$13,576,000**	**100**

Development Cost Information	Amount	% of Total
Phase I		
Site Acquisition Cost	$650,000	6
Site Improvement Cost	0	0
Construction Cost	7,838,000	68
Soft Costs	3,037,200	26
Total	**$11,525,200**	**100**
Phase II		
Site Acquisition Cost	$1,189,500	8
Site Improvement Cost	1,597,600	12
Construction Cost	7,164,600	53
Soft Costs	3,634,400	27
Total	**$13,586,100**	**100**

Peter Landon

Steinkamp/Ballogg Photography, Inc.

What do Fig Newtons, electric telegraph cables, pharmaceuticals, biotechnology, telescopes, shoes, oysters, and candy have in common with one of the nation's most prestigious universities? All of these items are associated with the history and future of the land that is occupied by University Park at MIT in Cambridge, Massachusetts. This 27-acre mixed-use, master-planned, research and development (R&D) park is situated on former marshland that was filled in and used for a wide range of industrial purposes. Auburn Court is a five-acre affordable housing component of this larger development.

Oyster fishing was perhaps one of the first industries on this stretch, but as the marshland was filled in, telescopes, candy, shoes, cable, and wires were all manufactured there. By the 20th century, most of the site was owned by Simplex Wire and Cable Company, a manufacturer of telegraph cables. Simplex left the site in the 1970s, and a decade later most of the area was vacant. Nearby was the F.A. Steam Bakery, birthplace of the Fig Newton, which later became home to a shoe manufacturer.

By 1982, MIT had assembled these parcels and issued a request for proposals to develop the site. With the goal of accelerating the transfer of technology to the commercial marketplace, the school sought to develop a corporate office/R&D park adjacent to its campus. MIT's objectives for this venture were to secure a good economic return for the MIT Endowment Fund, protect long-term campus growth, create employment opportunities for students and graduates, and provide collaborative advisory opportunities for faculty.

MIT signed the winning bidder, Forest City Enterprises, to a 20-year development agreement. Under the terms of this agreement, the firm will develop University Park using a series of 75-year ground leases, with each lease term to begin as each portion of the site is developed. Thus, under the terms of each lease, the properties gradually will all revert back to MIT, with all leases ending no later than 2078. Although no provision is included for lease renewal, no prohibition exists if MIT and Forest City choose to add one.

It took four years of master planning and the public approval process for MIT, Forest City, and the city of Cambridge to come to a consensus. The agreed-upon plans called for 1.3 million square feet of office/R&D space, a 210-room hotel and executive conference center, up to 150,000 square feet of retail space and restaurants, 650 rental housing units, four structured parking facilities for 2,800 cars, and seven acres of parkland. The University Park development team then chose Homeowner's Rehab, Inc. (HRI), to develop Auburn Court.

Like many affordable housing projects, funding came from a wide array of sources—more than a dozen in this case, including federal tax credits and loans, state grants, and private funding. The multiple funding sources made it difficult to coordinate institutional requirements and other administrative necessities: HRI had to work with many banks, lending institutions, MIT, and the city of Cambridge.

Auburn Court consists of three garden courtyard residential blocks and a small public park interconnected by a continuous pedestrian walkway. It was built in two phases, with 77 units in Phase I (designed by architectural firm Goody Clancy) and an additional 60 units (designed by ICON architecture, inc.) in Phase II. Half of all the units are reserved for those who earn less than 50 percent of the area median income.

Both phases consist of one-, two-, and three-bedroom units distributed among flats and duplexes. Typical buildings are three stories to reflect the scale of nearby homes. The buildings then graduate in size from four to six stories to frame the entrance to University Park. Nearly all the units have a terrace, porch, or balcony to provide private outdoor space. A variety of colors, materials, and building types gives the development the appearance of an older, well-established Cambridge neighborhood.

DEVELOPMENT TEAM

Master Planner
Forest City Boston
Cambridge, Massachusetts

Developer
Homeowner's Rehab, Inc.
Cambridge, Massachusetts

Architect
Goody Clancy
Boston, Massachusetts

ICON architecture, inc.
Boston, Massachusetts

Anton Grassl

Anton Grassl

RESIDENTS

Area Median Income (family of 4)	$80,800
Residents Served	50% of units serve those at up to 50% of AMI

LAND USE INFORMATION

	Phase I	Phase II
Site Area	4.3 acres	1.1 acres
Total Dwelling Units	77	60
Gross Project Density	18 units per acre	52.6 units per acre
Housing Type	Apartments	Apartments

RESIDENTIAL UNIT INFORMATION

Phase I

Unit Type	Floor Area (Sq. Ft.)	No. Built	Rent
1-Bedroom/1-Bath	610–750	15*	$862–1,900
2-Bedroom/1-Bath	800–1,014	43**	$1,022–2,350
3-Bedroom/1-Bath	1,100–1,350	19***	$1,324–2,550

* Three units are affordable to families at or below 50% of the AMI, and three are affordable to families at or below 90% of the AMI.

** Twenty-four units are affordable to families at or below 50% of the AMI, and four are affordable to families at or below 90% of AMI.

*** Twelve units are affordable to families at or below 50% of AMI.

Phase II

Unit Type	Floor Area (Sq. Ft.)	No. Built	Rent
1-Bedroom/1-Bath	625–645	12	$1,010–1,850
2-Bedroom/1-Bath	890–1,050	28*	$1,216–1,825
2-Bedroom/1.5-Bath	1,122–1,222	7*	$1,211–1,975
2-Bedroom/2-Bath	1,285	1*	$2,200
3-Bedroom/2-Bath	1,100–1,434	12**	$1,441–2,300

* Twenty of 35 two-bedroom units are affordable to families at or below 50% of the AMI.

** Ten units are affordable to families at or below 50% of the AMI, and two are affordable to families at or below 95% of the AMI.

Phase I

Gap Financing

City of Cambridge CDBG and Affordable Housing Trust

U.S. Department of Housing and Urban Development

Massachusetts Department of Housing and
   Community Development

Cambridge Neighborhood Housing Apartment Housing
   Services through Neighborhood Reinvestment

Construction Financing

Massachusetts Housing Financing Agency

Federal Home Loan Bank of Boston in conjunction with
   Cambridgeport Bank

Bridge Financing

Massachusetts Housing Partnership Fund

Permanent Financing

Massachusetts Housing Financing Agency

Massachusetts Government Land Bank

Limited Partner–Equity Investor

Federal National Mortgage Association

Low-Income Housing Tax Credits

U.S. Department of Housing and Urban Development

Rent Subsidies

Cambridge Housing Authority

U.S. Department of Housing and Urban Development

Predevelopment Funding

Local Initiatives Support Corporation

Community Economic Development Assistance Corporation

Neighborhood Reinvestment Corporation

Neighborhood Development Support Collaborative

The Hyams Foundation

The Riley Foundation

Lotus Development Corporation

Bank of Boston

The Boston Globe Foundation

Shawmut Bank N.A.

MIT (reduced sale price)

Phase II

Gap Financing

City of Cambridge CDBG

Cambridge Affordable Housing Trust

Massachusetts Department of Housing and Community
   Development HOME funds

Cambridge Neighborhood Apartment Housing Services

Neighborhood Reinvestment Corporation

Predevelopment Financing

Community Economic Development Assistance Corporation

Construction Financing

Massachusetts Housing Investment Corporation

Permanent First Mortgage Financing

Massachusetts Housing Partnership

Low-Income Housing Tax Credits

U.S. Department of Housing and Urban Development

Rent Subsidies

Cambridge Housing Authority

U.S. Department of Housing and Urban Development

In-Kind Contributions/Grants

Cambridge Electric Light Company (NSTAR)

Verizon/Cable Vision

SMOC/Energy Star

Anton Grassl

Anton Grassl

In the early 1990s, Chelsea Court was a single-room occupancy (SRO) building in mid-Manhattan on the verge of collapse. All but vacant, the building's only use was as a crack den. The city of New York first condemned the building because it had become structurally unstable and then in a separate action seized the property for nonpayment of taxes.

As a result of various deed restrictions imposed by government agencies, any new development on the property had to be predominantly low-income housing. Fed up by the poor condition of the building, the 17th Street Block Association, the neighborhood block association, formed an alliance with the New York City Department of Housing Preservation and Development (HPD) and Palladia, Inc. (at the time, Project Return Foundation) to redevelop the property. Palladia then bought the property from the city for $1.00.

Palladia, Inc., has a long track record of providing a variety of social services, including permanent housing, to New Yorkers. Since its founding in 1970, Palladia has helped people cope with problems relating to substance abuse, homelessness, HIV, past criminal records, mental illness, and domestic violence. Palladia had originally planned to house exclusively those with special needs such as people with substance abuse histories at Chelsea Court. The 17th Street Block Association, however, was less than receptive, and the combination of rapid upzoning of nearby residential stock and the rapid gentrification of the neighborhood led Palladia to choose to house a different set of tenants at Chelsea Court. Now 14 of Chelsea Court's 18 studio apartments provide homes to the formerly homeless. The remaining four units serve low-income residents. Palladia also ensured that each tenant in the building has access to on-site support services.

The 17th Street Block Association's role in the development did not end with the selection of Palladia. It became actively involved as a result of members' concerns about safety. Palladia made several presentations to the block association and shared with them design plans, information about funding, and the potential tenant profile. The block association was also solicited for recommendations of individuals to rent some of the units. Palladia also provides 24-hour security coverage for the building.

Funding for the project came from a number of different sources, starting with capital funding from the New York City Department of Housing Preservation and Development Supportive Housing Loan Program. The U.S. Department of Housing and Urban Development provided funding for support services and rental subsidies administered by HPD. Palladia also partnered with the Enterprise Social Investment Corporation to syndicate tax credits from HPD's federal LIHTC program.

Architect Louise Braverman's keen vision transformed the dilapidated 35-unit, one-toilet, water-damaged, rat-infested building into an award-winning apartment building. The entire interior of the building was gutted, and new structural, electrical, mechanical, and fire protection systems were added. Braverman used the color blue as a design theme that guides visitors through the building. It starts as a "blue ribbon" of translucent glass at the streetfront that greets people as they enter the building. Inside, the blue theme is translated into a series of metallic blue display niches along a public corridor. The corridor and the blue theme lead visitors past a metallic blue and green security desk and up the chromatically sequenced glazed concrete masonry blocks in the stairwells. An additional amenity, a rooftop garden, provides a comfortable and private space for tenants to relax in the sun. For Braverman's efforts, the project was a winner of the 2003 AIA New York State Design Award of Merit.

Area Median Income (family of 4)	$51,900
Residents Served	78% of units to serve residents with no income; 22% of units to serve those at less than 50% of AMI

LAND USE INFORMATION

Site Area	11,000 square feet
Total Dwelling Units	18
Housing Type	Apartments

RESIDENTIAL UNIT INFORMATION

Unit Type	Floor Area (Sq. Ft.)	No. Built	Rent (1st Month)
Studio	240–345	14	$675 (reserved for those who earn less than 50% of the area median income)
Studio	240–345	4	$563 (reserved for those with no income)

©Scott Frances

FUNDING SOURCES

Capital Funding Sources	Amount	% of Total
NYC HPD	$1,610,600	44.5
Enterprise Social Investment Corporation: raised equity from private investors by the syndication of federal LIHTCs allocated by HPD	1,306,600	36.1
HUD Supportive Housing Program	400,000	11.0
Purchase money mortgage to HPD based on appraisal of property	305,000	8.4
Total	**$3,622,200**	**100.0**

Program Funding and Other Funding Sources		
HUD Supportive Housing Program (Services Funding)	$ 496,900	
New York City Department of Homeless Services	$ 222,400	
HUD Section 8 Moderate Rental Subsidies (10-year period)	$1,025,300	

DEVELOPMENT COSTS

Development Cost Information	Amount	% of Total
Site Acquisition	$ 305,000	8.4
Site Improvement/Construction	2,025,400	55.9
Public Improvements	0	0
Project-Related Soft Costs	706,300	19.5
Syndication-Related Costs	27,500	0.8
Reserves	558,100	15.4
Total	**$3,622,300**	**100.0**

DEVELOPMENT TEAM

Developer
Palladia, Inc.
New York, New York

Architect
Louise Braverman, AIA
New York, New York

Builder
P&P Contracting Corporation
New York, New York

Consulting Engineers
Goldreich Engineering, PC
New York, New York

Kallen & Lemelson, Consulting Engineers, LLP
New York, New York

Louise Braverman, Architect

Located next to LeMoyne-Owen College, a historically black university in Memphis, Tennessee, College Park has reinvented itself. College Park presents another example of the power of HOPE VI funds in improving public housing. Originally the site of LeMoyne Gardens, a public housing project built between 1941 and 1943 by the Federal Housing Authority and the Memphis Housing Authority (MHA), College Park has replaced a series of identical reinforced concrete and brick multi-family buildings with a vibrant mix of housing types, architectural styles, and colors. Lacking private open spaces and having only two roads run through the 27- acre property, the original project was typical of many government housing projects from that time period.

The location near LeMoyne-Owen College was chosen because planners thought that residents would be able to build off the cultural and civic functions of the college. The MHA even named the project LeMoyne Gardens to reflect this connection. But despite the best intentions of planners and architects, LeMoyne Gardens was not able to live up to these high expectations. By 1995, almost 36 percent of the project sat vacant. In 1999, the MHA entered into a master development agreement with LeMoyne Redevelopment, LLC, a joint venture of Integral Properties, LLC, and Mid-City Urban, LLC. Through this partnership, the development team was able to secure a $47 million HOPE VI grant. Together, this team built 341 family rental units and a community center. Services under the partnership ended in October 2003. At that point, the MHA took on the role of developer to develop for-sale houses, the final component of the project. Additional funds for the project came from the Tennessee LIHTC program, city of Memphis capital funds, and private sector investments. In a symbolic break from the past, residents voted to change the name from LeMoyne Gardens to College Park. The new name retains a link to LeMoyne-Owen College but helps the residents of College Park to

chart a very different course from that of LeMoyne Gardens. Today, the neighborhood is characterized by single-family homes, quadruplexes, duplexes, and rowhouses, all built of wood frame construction. At 36 acres, it is nine acres larger than its predecessor. Each multifamily building is designed to blend into a neighborhood of freestanding single-family homes. The preservation of mature trees during construction and the wide porches that adorn the fronts and sides of many buildings help to create a friendly and inviting streetscape. Buildings at the center of the development are oriented around a large green space that further adds to an inviting public realm.

Ninety percent of the units are reserved for those with incomes at 60 percent of Memphis's area median income, with rents set at one-third of household income. Of the 411 units, 80 are allocated for senior housing, 371 units are rental units, and 40 are for-sale housing.

Torti Gallas and Partners

Area Median Income (family of 4)	$51,000
Residents Served	90% of units serve those at 60% of AMI

LAND USE INFORMATION

Site Area	36 acres
Total Dwelling Units	411
Gross Project Density	11.4 units per acre
Housing Type	Planned community

RESIDENTIAL UNIT INFORMATION

Unit Type	Floor Area (Sq. Ft.)	No. Built	Rent (1st Month)
Senior-Only Rental Units			
1-Bedroom/1-Bath (units in a three-story elevator building)	613	68	$644
2-Bedroom (units in six duplexes)	904	24	$774
Family Rental Units			
1-Bedroom/1-Bath Walkup	736	40	$644
2-Bedroom/1-Bath Walkup	904	128	$774
3-Bedroom/2.5-Bath Townhouse	1,350	70	$894
3-Bedroom/2-Bath Flat (handicapped accessible)	1,309	4	$894
4-Bedroom/2.5-Bath Townhouse	1,533	17	$997
4-Bedrooms/2-Bath Flat (handicapped accessible)	1,472	2	$997
3-Bedroom Homeownership Units	1,500–1,800	36	$73–$77,000
4-Bedroom Homeownership Units	1,500–1,800	34	$73–$77,000

FUNDING SOURCES

Funding Source	Amount	% of Total
HUD	$47,281,000	76
City of Memphis	5,615,000	9
Social Service matching funding from CDBG funds—$675,000		
Acquisition funds from Capital Improvement Program funds—$1,000,000		
City Downpayment Assistance from CDBG funds—$690,000		
Infrastructure/Project Reserves from CIP funds—$3,250,000)		
Tennessee Housing Development Agency LIHTCs	5,000,000	8
Private Investment (sale of LIHTCs)	4,300,000	7
Total	**$62,196,000**	**100**

DEVELOPMENT COSTS

Development Cost Information	Amount	% of Total
Project Management	$2,304,800	3.8
Construction Management	6,533,900	10.7
Architecture/Engineering	609,500	1.0
Legal Fees	864,100	1.4
Other Planning and Professional Fees	1,094,800	1.8
Demolition/Remediation	1,330,600	2.2
Acquisition	46,400	0.0
Site Improvements	5,115,800	8.4
Construction of Dwelling Units	25,077,700	41.1
Non-Dwelling-Unit Equipment	93,000	0.2
Community Center Construction	4,265,500	7.0
Relocation/Reoccupancy	258,600	0.4
Tax Credit Costs	66,500	0.1
Developer's Fees	1,218,100	2.0
Other Costs	4,744,400	7.8
Reserves	1,630,800	2.7
Community and Support Services	4,086,200	6.7
Grant Administration	1,631,800	2.7
Total	**$60,972,500**	**100.0**

Steve Hall © Hedrich Blessing

DEVELOPMENT TEAM

Developer
LeMoyne Redevelopment, LLC
Memphis Housing Authority
Memphis, Tennessee

Architect
Torti Gallas and Partners
Silver Spring, Maryland

Builder
Beazer Homes
Tempe, Arizona

Landscape Architect
Pickering Firm, Inc.
Memphis, Tennessee

Steve Hall © Hedrich Blessing

Like the rest of the nation, southern California faces a growing shortage of affordable housing. The city of Los Angeles Housing Authority's waiting list for public housing increased by 25 percent between 2002 and 2003. With a 36-month wait, the city estimates that the housing authority is meeting only 8 percent of the need. For the Los Angeles area, the median income is $19,000 less than the income needed to buy a median-priced home.

Bordering Los Angeles, the city of Santa Monica faces the same housing shortages. In addition to addressing the regional housing crisis, Santa Monica is also deeply committed to issues of sustainability and has even developed a sustainable city plan to help guide the city. The plan has led the city to develop a number of innovative and environmentally sensitive policies, including strong energy efficiency requirements for city-owned buildings.

The city has set an ambitious goal of trying to get every qualified city building "LEED silver certified." LEED (Leadership in Energy and Environmental Design) certification is a voluntary rating system through which buildings of all types can be compared based on the degree to which they incorporate environmentally friendly elements into their design. Using a point system based on five criteria (indoor environmental quality, materials and resources, sustainable sites, water efficiency, and energy and atmosphere), LEED offers four levels of certification: Certified, Silver, Gold, and Platinum (the highest).

With its environmentally friendly focus, the city of Santa Monica partnered with the nonprofit Community Corporation of Santa Monica (CCSM) to develop housing that is both affordable and sustainable. Because energy costs are among the highest household expenses after rent or mortgage payments, matching affordable housing to green design presents a strong, tangible benefit for tenants, in addition to helping the environment.

After a three-year design and development process, Colorado Court is home to 44 energy-efficient studios in a five-story apartment complex. The units are cozy, with 375 square feet per apartment, but ten-foot high ceilings and extensive use of natural light give each studio an open feeling. The residential units are built over a 20-space parking garage. Building over the parking garage has allowed the property to reduce the overall level of impermeable surface on site. The project also includes a ground-level community room and outdoor courtyards.

Designed by architectural firm Pugh + Scarpa, every aspect of the building reflects awareness for environmental issues and concerns. Perhaps the most striking feature of the building is its front facade. More than 200 two-foot-by-five-foot solar panels cover the front and top of the building. These panels form an eye-catching, shimmering wall of indigo blue. Landscaping around the building consists of the original palm trees from the site and drought-tolerant plants, all watered efficiently through a drip irrigation system.

The solar panels work with a natural gas microturbine generator to supply the majority of energy for the building. The natural gas microturbine uses a heat recovery system to provide hot water for the entire building. Colorado Court was designed (based on June 2001 energy rates) to produce an energy savings of up to $10,000 a year and supply almost 100 percent of the building's electrical needs.

Careful attention to the placement and siting of the building has created a natural ventilation system. The building's location, orientation, and shape take into account prevailing winds and exposure to the sun. As a result, only one small section of the office space on the ground floor is equipped with air conditioning. The design of windows further maximizes both ventilation and light levels; for example, special attention was paid to shading and window glazes to mediate southern and western exposures.

City officials also worked on behalf of the project to lobby for changes to the state's electrical net metering regulations. Net metering is a means of selling the excess energy generated on site by alternative energy sources to back to energy utility companies. CCSM and the city of Santa Monica intended for Colorado Court to sell its excess energy generated during the day to pay for energy consumed at night. Before the project was constructed, the state of California had regulations that only allowed net metering for systems generating a maximum of ten kilowatts. At 30 kilowatts, Colorado Court exceeded these maximums. To help change this law, the city successfully teamed up with state senator Sheila Kuehl to encourage the state assembly to pass legislation allowing for net metering of projects generating up to one megawatt (1,000 kilowatts).

To the disappointment of CCSM, the new net metering regulation prohibits projects with two or more sources of energy from selling energy back to utility companies. Because Colorado Court has both the solar panels and the gas turbine generator, it is not eligible for the net metering program. Nonetheless, the two combined systems produce more energy than is consumed. Excess energy does flow back to the electrical grid, but CCSM cannot recoup the financial benefits offered by net metering.

Although the city of Santa Monica provided both the land and the majority of financing, additional funding came from a number of different sources. CCSM entered into an 87-year ground lease with the city to develop the property and is the owner of the improvements to the property. Rebates from various environmental measures are helping to reduce the city's permanent loans, and the California Department of Housing and Community Development's Multifamily Housing Program and the Federal Home Loan Bank's Affordable Housing Program have also provided funding. Low debt service requirements for the project have helped to keep rents extremely low and affordable for tenants. On top of traditional construction expenses, green measures added an additional $542,000 to the overall cost of the building. These additional costs were covered through government programs that encourage green building, including $400,000 from Regional Energy Efficiency Initiative funds that were administered through a partnership between the city of Santa Monica and the California Energy Coalition, a nonprofit organization that promotes strategies to maximize efficient use of energy. The state of California photovoltaic buydown program provided another $124,000, and the Southern California Gas Company supplied $18,000.

For the city of Santa Monica, Colorado Court became a demonstration project to show the possibilities of good environmental design and the importance of incorporating alternative energy sources into new developments. The city was a very strong advocate for the project and was able to help Colorado Court overcome hurdles caused by its employment of new technologies. The solar panels on the front of the building, for example, required special consideration from the fire safety inspector because such architectural features are still very new to the area. Such hurdles allowed city officials to examine how to help the entitlement process take into account the innovations created by green building technologies.

Although Colorado Court has achieved its primary goal of providing high-quality affordable housing, it also serves as an example of the promise green building strategies have for respecting the environment and bringing greater awareness to environmental systems. Colorado Court is currently in the process of attaining LEED certification. In 2003, the American Institute of Architects voted it one of its top ten green projects. When the project first opened, all units were fully occupied and 3,000 people were on a waiting list.

Sam Newberg/Joe Urban, Inc.

DEVELOPMENT TEAM

Developer
Community Corporation of Santa Monica
Santa Monica, California

Funders/Consultants
City of Santa Monica
Santa Monica, California

State of California
Department of Housing and Community Development
Sacramento, California

Architect
Pugh + Scarpa
Santa Monica, California

Builder
Ruiz Brothers Construction Company, Inc.
Commerce, California

Pugh + Scarpa

Sam Newberg/Joe Urban, Inc.

Source	Amount	% of Total
City of Santa Monica	$4,009,000	68
Multifamily Housing Program Loan	1,629,000	28
FHLB (AHP program)	207,000	4
Bank of America Grant	5,000	0
Rebates for Green Measures	21,000	0
Total	**$5,871,000**	100
Rebates for Green Measures to pay down city of Santa Monica loan	$330,000	6

DEVELOPMENT COSTS

Development Cost Information	Amount	% of Total
Site Acquisition (ground lease with city of Santa Monica)	$0	0
Site Improvement/Construction Costs (including public improvements)	$4,674,000	80
Soft Costs	$1,197,000	20
Total	**$5,871,000**	100

Sam Newberg/Joe Urban, Inc.

Sam Newberg/Joe Urban, Inc.

Situated in a middle-class urban neighborhood, Dove Street Independent Housing offers one-bedroom apartments to formerly homeless men and women living with AIDS and other disabilities. Capital Hill Improvement Corporation (CHIC), the project's developer, faced many funding challenges. The project was developed with the expectation that LIHTCs would be part of the funding package. Those funds, however, never materialized, and the developer was forced to forgo its development fee and default on some of its payments.

The development team also faced some challenges securing a suitable site for the project. When the team's initial application to New York's Homeless Housing Assistance Program (HHAP) was unsuccessful because of the great competition for funds, the developers were in jeopardy of losing the site chosen for the project. To secure the site until funding became available, individual members of the development team fronted the necessary cash out of their own pockets.

The development team also lacked the funds necessary to prepare the architectural plans required for a project application. An architecture firm, Dorgan Architecture & Planning, completed all the preliminary work for the project on a contingent basis.

The project's financial problems were solved when it received funding from HHAP. HHAP provides funds to nonprofit developers who develop housing for the homeless or those who cannot find housing without assistance programs. Previous recipients of these funds have built housing for a wide range of homeless people, including youth, the elderly, victims of domestic violence, and people with AIDS. CHIC also obtained money from the Capital District Community Loan Fund, a nonprofit lender that supports community development projects in the capital region of New York state. In addition, support for operations is provided through a U.S. Department of Housing and Urban Development Housing Opportunities for People with AIDS grant.

Realizing that residents in the surrounding neighborhood might be concerned about the project's intended tenants, the developers sought neighborhood input at every stage of the process, from planning all the way through to completion. As a result, the project received unanimous support from neighbors while other communities throughout Albany were rejecting similar projects. Since its completion in 1997, neighbors continue to support the project and have helped build a community and support network for the residents.

Location in the historic Center Square/Hudson Park neighborhood complicated the design process but yielded a higher quality product that has satisfied all stakeholders. The historic designation of the neighborhood meant developers were unable to stray from proposed plans without long authorization processes; the new buildings had to match the 19th-century rowhouses that characterize the area. Both the local and state preservation offices regulated plans and construction.

Photos: Dorgan Architecture & Planning

This process benefited the neighborhood greatly. The long review process and detailed plans required by the preservation boards ensured that every detail the community saw on the plans made its way to construction and that no surprises arose. The final product is a series of eight rowhouses with fully modern interiors and exteriors that emulate the 19th-century design that typifies the neighborhood.

Dorgan Architecture & Planning consulted closely with local AIDS advocates, people living with AIDS, and their caregivers to determine specific housing needs. As a result of this research and collaboration, two key features were included in the design. The first, in-unit laundry facilities, allows residents with AIDS to complete their daily chores without having to leave the unit and without having to enter a public laundry, where the spread of viruses and bacteria could occur. The second, ample storage, has been provided so that residents can store their various medicines and medical equipment inconspicuously.

Additional interior details ensure that when a cure to AIDS is found, the units can be converted to accessible units for the handicapped. All units conform to the Americans with Disabilities Act and have kitchens that are designed with wheelchair-bound individuals in mind. Other features include sloped risers, grab bars, and railings, and visual alarms are available for the hearing impaired.

The completed project has successfully provided affordable homes for formerly homeless men and women suffering from AIDS and other disabilities. Stable housing conditions allow residents to focus their attention on other issues. Renting for a minimum of "shelter rent" and a maximum of 30 percent of an individual's income, Dove Street Independent Housing has helped individuals begin to manage their disease and improve their lives.

DEVELOPMENT TEAM

Developer
Capital Hill Improvement Corporation
(no longer in existence)

Architect
Dorgan Architecture & Planning
Storrs, Connecticut

Consultant
AIDS Council of Northeastern New York
Schenectady, New York

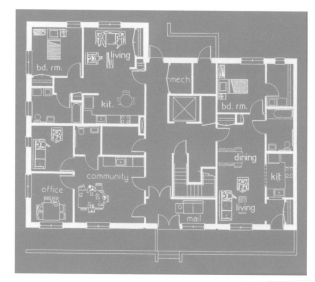

Dorgan Architecture & Planning

RESIDENTS

Area Median Income (family of 4)	$59,800
Residents Served	100% of units serve those at 30% of AMI

LAND USE INFORMATION

Site Area	0.25 acre
Total Dwelling Units	8
Gross Project Density	32 units per acre
Housing Type	Single-family rowhouses

RESIDENTIAL UNIT INFORMATION

Unit Type	Floor Area (Sq. Ft.)	No. Built	Rent
1-Bedroom	700	8	Shelter rent or 30% of income

FUNDING SOURCES

Funding Source	Amount	% of Total
New York State HHAP	$670,000	89
Capital District Community Loan Fund	80,000	11
Total	**$750,000**	**100**

DEVELOPMENT COSTS

Development Cost Information	Amount	% of Total
Site Acquisition	$38,000	5
Site Improvement/Construction	645,000	86
Total Soft Costs	67,000	9
Total	**$750,000**	**100**

Dorgan Architecture & Planning

Howard University and its adjacent neighborhood, LeDroit Park, share a rich and textured history. In 1867, shortly after the emancipation of the slaves, Howard University was founded with a mission to uplift and educate both freed slaves and those African Americans fortunate enough to have been born free. Six years later, Amzi L. Barber, one of the university trustees, purchased 55 acres from the school and resigned from the board. On this land, he planned and developed LeDroit Park in 1879. Named after Barber's father-in-law, LeDroit Park was originally a whites-only gated community of well-crafted homes built in a number of different styles, including Italian villa, Gothic revival, Queen Anne, and Italianate.

The segregation in LeDroit Park was short lived, and by 1894, it was home to its first of many African American residents. The turn of the century brought more black residents into this neighborhood, who were to include many prominent people—Paul Lawrence Dunbar, Ralph Bunche, Edward Brooke, and Walter Washington, the District of Columbia's first mayor elected under home rule.

The decades following World War II witnessed a drastic decline in the neighborhood, a decline mirrored by many other inner-city neighborhoods around the nation. LeDroit Park became characterized by high crime rates, abandoned buildings, poorly maintained properties and services, and a dearth of neighborhood amenities. Even the 1970 placement of LeDroit Park on the National Park Service's National Register of Historic Places did little to turn around the neighborhood.

By the 1990s, about 18 percent of the neighborhood sat vacant. This problem was exacerbated by Howard University's plans to expand its health facilities. During the 1970s and 1980s, the university had purchased 30 properties for the proposed expansion. The expansion never occurred, and the properties sat vacant, further contributing to the decline of this historic neighborhood.

With the expansion plans scrapped but still owning a number of neighborhood properties, Howard University embarked on an ambitious partnership with the Fannie Mae Foundation, the Fannie Mae Corporation, and Riggs Bank to reenvision a 150-block area around the university. This partnership led to the Howard University/LeDroit Park revitalization initiative. Based on community involvement at all levels, from individual residents to investors, the initiative outlined a three-part improvement program comprising a land use plan, a streetscape plan, and a housing plan.

The two-acre residential component served to jump-start the larger revitalization effort. In the first phase, noted architecture firm Sorg and Associates renovated 28 historic single-family rowhouses and constructed 12 new homes, each accommodating from two to five bedrooms. The architect designed five prototypes that re-created elements of the original dwellings to retain the neighborhood's character. Later phases of the project increased the number of renovated and constructed homes.

Built for moderate-income families, 30 percent of the units are available for sale to persons making half the area median income. To encourage them to live in the area, Howard offered university employees a 7 percent subsidy that made it possible for buyers to make downpayments as low as 3 percent of the purchase price.

The streetscape plan improved the neighborhood's aesthetic appeal while resolving security issues. Features include shade trees along new brick sidewalks, traditional post lighting, and special paved areas that incorporate quotations and anecdotes by and about famous residents.

The land use plan included ideas to create the first national African American museum, restore the historic Howard Theater, build an African American jazz center, and transform McMillan Reservoir into a recreational area with new picnic grounds, bike trails, and playing fields.

The Howard University/LeDroit Park initiative represents a key turning point for two major aspects of urban redevelopment. First, the initiative offers a new template of how urban universities can embrace neighboring communities and work with them toward mutually beneficial goals. Second, the initiative is a step in the revitalization of one of the nation's first African American historic districts. The initiative has preserved historic buildings and created new housing on vacant lots that reflect the historic character of the neighborhood.

The success of the initiative has led the Fannie Mae Foundation to use LeDroit Park as a model for its America's Living Communities Plan. The plan seeks to invest $3 billion in 300 neighborhoods over ten years, with the goal of re-creating the successes and implementing the lessons learned from LeDroit Park.

Sorg and Associates

DEVELOPMENT TEAM

Developers
Howard University
Washington, D.C.

Fannie Mae Foundation
Washington, D.C.

Fannie Mae Corporation
Washington, D.C.

Architect
Sorg and Associates
Washington, D.C.

Builder
Essex Construction
Oxon Hill, Maryland

Landscape Architect
Oehme, van Sweden & Associates, Inc.
Washington, D.C.

Area Median Income (family of 4)	$91,500 (2002)
Residents Served	30% of units serve those at 50% of AMI

Site Area	2 acres
Total Dwelling Units	40
Gross Project Density	20 units per acre
Housing Type	Single-family rowhouses

Unit Type	Floor Area (Sq. Ft.)	No. Built	Sale Price
3-Bedroom/1.5-Bath	1,030–1,160	3 rehab	$105,000–107,500
3-Bedroom/1.5-Bath	1,258	2 rehab	$105,500
2-Bedroom/1-Bath	784	2 rehab	$ 89,500
3-Bedroom/1.5-Bath	1,700	9 rehab	$139,000–173,000
3-Bedroom/1.5-Bath	1,600	12 new	$142,000–175,000

Sorg and Associates

Funding Source	Amount	% of Total
Howard University		
University-Owned Houses and Lots in LeDroit Park	$1,375,000	12
Employer-Assisted Homeownership Program	500,000	4
Fannie Mae Corporation		
LeDroit Park Neighborhood Market Study	15,000	0.1
Consultant Services	25,000	0.2
Technical Consulting and Professional Support	200,000	2
Predevelopment Loan to Howard University	300,000	3
Employer-Assisted Homeownership Program	500,000	4
Construction Financing Participation	2,500,000	22
DCHFA (targeted area builder bonds purchased for mortgages for Howard University units; 5.9% for income-eligible families in 1998–1999)	5,000,000	43
Fannie Mae Foundation		
Comprehensive Land Use Plan Study; Cultural District Study; 150-Block Field Survey of Public Space; Infrastructure Needs; Streetscape Redesign	1,150,000	10
Total	**$11,565,000**	**100**

Development Cost Information	Amount	% of Total
Site Acquisition	$1,375,000	24
Soft Costs	1,450,000	25
Construction Costs	3,000,000	51
Total	**$5,825,000**	**100**

Public Improvements Not Yet Completed

District of Columbia Department of Public Works	$5,000,000
U.S. Department of Transportation	$500,000

The thought of a municipal housing project acting as a tool for economic and neighborhood development would have been considered contradictory not too many years ago, but now cities are discovering that serving the needs of vulnerable populations can actually improve neighborhoods. The La Cascada II apartment building has helped to turn around the dangerous Sunnyslope area in Phoenix, Arizona, while simultaneously providing homes for seniors. Before redevelopment, the lot on which La Cascada II now sits was home to a deteriorated duplex. Gang members and vagrants frequented the duplex, and neighbors reported seeing many criminal activities taking place there. The owners of the property received several zoning violation citations for graffiti and overgrown vegetation. The condition of this lot made a dangerous neighborhood even more dangerous.

Neighbors welcomed the city's decision to build housing on the lot, because it meant one less place for gang members to conduct their criminal activities. The resulting project, La Cascada II, is the second phase of a seniors' housing development funded by the city of Phoenix. Both phases of the La Cascada project were part of a city strategy to transform neighborhoods through housing. Other improvement efforts in Sunnyslope involved a series of strategic acquisitions and condemnations of land to reduce crime on abandoned or neglected properties.

La Cascada and the adjacent city-owned Sunnyslope Manor provide independent living for seniors on a tight budget. La Cascada II is only for people age 55 and older whose income is between 20 and 55 percent of the area median income. Funding for La Cascada II came from general obligation funds that were part of an allocation stemming from a bond election held in 1988.

Great care went into the design of this building. Todd & Associates, the architectural firm responsible for designing the structure, had to create a building that would protect residents from crime, meet standards for accessibility of the Americans with Disabilities Act (ADA), and still be a pleasant place to live. To meet these goals, the architects had many discussions with residents and the people in the surrounding community.

The apartment is constructed with masonry and stucco—chosen for their long-term durability. The exterior is a rich, warm palate of brick, reddish brown, and pale yellow, a color scheme common in the Southwest that complements the adobe buildings in the region.

Flexible spaces for both public and private use are primary features of La Cascada II. A large multipurpose room next to the main entry opens onto a landscaped central courtyard. Curved benches, a stone waterfall, and a barbecue create a community gathering point. Each of the 36 units has a covered balcony that faces this courtyard. Large massed walls on the exterior of the building help regulate the temperature both within the courtyard and for the building as a whole. The walls absorb heat during the day and release it at night. Small openings in the concrete admit natural light along corridors and promote air circulation throughout the facade.

Based on residents' suggestions, each unit has generous storage space, a full kitchen, a bathroom, a living room, and a bedroom with a walk-in-closet. An elevator provides access to all three floors, and each of the 36 units in the building is accessible in accord with the ADA.

Photos: Todd & Associates, Inc.

Area Median Income (family of 4)	$58,300
Residents Served	100% of units to serve 20% to 55% of AMI for people age 55 years and up

LAND USE INFORMATION

Site Area	1.08 acres
Total Dwelling Units	36
Gross Project Density	33.3 units per acre
Housing Type	Apartments

RESIDENTIAL UNIT INFORMATION

Unit Type	Floor Area (Sq. Ft.)	No. Built	Rent (1st Month)
1-Bedroom/1-Bath (second and third floors)	700	18	$335
1-Bedroom/1-Bath (first floor)	700	18	$345

FUNDING SOURCES

Funding Source	Amount	% of Total
General Obligation Bonds	$4,528,938	100
Total	**$4,528,938**	**100**

DEVELOPMENT COSTS

Development Cost Information	Amount	% of Total
Site Acquisition	$100,900	2
Site Improvement/Construction	3,826,000	85
EAS Department Fees	246,300	5
Architectural Fees	355,800	8
Total	**$4,529,000**	**100**

Todd & Associates, Inc.

Todd & Associates, Inc.

Developer
City of Phoenix Housing Department
Phoenix, Arizona

Architect
Todd & Associates, Inc.
Phoenix, Arizona

Builder
Woods Construction Company
Mesa, Arizona

Todd & Associates, Inc.

Indianapolis-based Partners in Housing Development Corporation (PIHDC) is dedicated to its mission "to create or cause to be created affordable housing for people with special needs." PIHDC was initially intended to be a subsidiary of Indiana Cares, a social service organization for people with AIDS. The agency began with the goal of securing a HUD Housing Opportunities for Persons with AIDS grant for Indiana Cares, but with the success of this first project in 1993, the development team decided to break from Indiana Cares and specialize in creating more housing for people with special needs.

For the team at PIHDC, "special needs" is an umbrella term encompassing physical, emotional, mental, and life-stage conditions. PIHDC offers programs, services, and housing for people with mental illness, substance abuse issues, AIDS/HIV, physical or developmental disabilities, and survivors of domestic abuse. Its program of supportive housing gives residents direct access to social services and helps them to gain the skills necessary to confront the issues that contributed to their homelessness.

Mozingo Place is located at the corner of 10th and Rural streets in a historic building constructed in the 1920s. The streetfront commercial facade serves both as a reminder of this intersection's past as a neighborhood hub and as a harbinger of the potential development and economic growth to come. Before the development of Mozingo Place, the building sat vacant, quietly deteriorating.

The years of neglect for such a historic building in such a visible location had the neighborhood residents clamoring for action. The intersection where the building sits also represents the confluence of four different neighborhood organizations. Because of PIHDC's track record and by working individually with these organizations, PIHDC was able to gain the support of all four neighborhood organizations for Mozingo Place.

Mozingo Place is an excellent example of a win-win situation: the adaptive use of this historic building contributes to the economic revitalization of the once-thriving 10th Street corridor while providing affordable housing for extremely low-income households. The 22 efficiency and one-bedroom rental units serve residents whose income level is 30 percent of the area median income, specifically addressing the needs of those with mental and physical disabilities and helping the formerly homeless.

Named after one of PIHDC's founding members, Todd Mozingo, Mozingo Place consists of two buildings. The historic building faces the intersection of 10th and Rural streets with 7,500 square feet of ground-level retail space topped with 12 stories of residences. A new building created behind the historic building houses the remaining ten units, a community meeting space, and laundry facilities. In between is a courtyard that serves as an escape from the noise and activity along the revitalized 10th Street corridor, providing both privacy and access to green space for the residents.

URS Corporation served as both project architect and landscape architect. Its design balanced the historic character of the original building with the contemporary design of the new building. An interior courtyard is the unifying element that connects the two buildings.

Living up to its name, PIHDC created many partnerships in the area to provide high-quality social support services to the residents of Mozingo Place. Two of its strongest partnerships are with two of its commercial tenants: the Mental Health Association of Marion County and the Community Choice Federal Credit Union. The mental health association has offices in the commercial section of the historic building and uses ten of the units in Mozingo Place, allowing it to provide comprehensive case management services for its clients. The credit union provides an array of basic financial services such as affordable loans and financial education for low-income community members. It seeks to provide an alternative to the high-cost and often predatory financial services commonly found in lower-income areas.

Developer
Partners in Housing Development Corporation
Indianapolis, Indiana

Architect and Landscape Architect
URS Corporation
Indianapolis, Indiana

Builder
Brandt Construction, Inc.
Indianapolis, Indiana

URS Corporation

RESIDENTS

Area Median Income (family of 4)	$62,900
Residents Served	100% of units serve those at 30% of AMI

LAND USE INFORMATION

Site Area	0.77 acre
Total Dwelling Units	22
Gross Project Density	28.6 units per acre
Housing Type	Multifamily/special needs

RESIDENTIAL UNIT INFORMATION

Unit Type	Floor Area (Sq. Ft.)	No. Built	Rent (1st Month)
Efficiency	309	3 new	$254–336
Efficiency	309	6 rehab	$254–336
1-Bedroom	470	7 new	$255–361
1-Bedroom	470	6 rehab	$255–361

FUNDING SOURCES

Source	Amount	% of Total
LIHTC Equity	$1,250,000	42.6
Neighborhood Assistance Program Tax Credits	85,000	3.0
Historic Tax Credits	115,000	4.0
Permanent Mortgage	180,000	6.1
Community Development Block Grants	350,000	12.0
HUD Housing Opportunities for People with AIDS Grant	150,000	5.1
HOME–Indianapolis	250,000	8.6
AHP Federal Home Loan Bank	165,000	5.6
Historic Landmarks Foundation of Indiana Grant	2,800	0
Indianapolis Foundation Grant	150,000	5.1
United Way Grant	200,000	6.8
GAP General Partner Note	33,650	1.1
Total	**$2,931,450**	**100.0**

DEVELOPMENT COSTS

Development Cost Information	Amount	% of Total
Site Acquisition	$110,000	4
Abatement	15,000	1
Rehabilitation	2,023,000	69
Appliances	25,000	1
Architect	158,800	5
Project Manager/Consultant	35,000	1
Engineering/Survey	10,000	0
Title and Recording	7,500	0
Legal	47,200	2
Insurance	8,500	0
IHFA Fee	8,000	0
Other Fees	10,000	0
Appraisal	5,000	0
Environmental Report	4,500	0
Accounting	5,000	0
Taxes	1,500	0
Developer's Fee	360,000	12
Operating Reserve	50,000	2
Rent-Up Reserve	55,000	2
Total	**$2,939,000**	**100**

URS Corporation

Not long ago, the neighborhood of Hope Gardens near downtown Nashville was unable to live up to its name. Drug use and related crime, violence, and prostitution had residents terrified. In 2002, Nashville metropolitan police logged more than 2,300 service calls for just a half-mile portion of Hope Gardens.

Even though this neighborhood has an enviable location, few were able to see how promising the neighborhood is. Residents of Hope Gardens are in walking distance of a farmers' market, grocery and drug stores, downtown Nashville, and Bicentennial Mall State Park. Recognizing the potential of this neighborhood and the need for higher-quality affordable housing, a nonprofit firm, Affordable Housing Resources (AHR), worked in a coalition with the city, the state, other nonprofit agencies, and for-profit developers to improve life in Hope Gardens.

In the 1990s, this coalition built 50 new affordable homes. The predominant buyers were single mothers with an average of two children. Although the project was a great success in providing homeownership opportunities to those in great need, it did little to change the neighborhood. To really change the neighborhood, AHR felt it was necessary to bring in a diverse range of people with varying levels of income.

Row 8.9n is one of the first residential projects in Nashville to combine subsidized housing with market-rate units to create a project rich in style and economic and cultural diversity. Thirty-eight percent of the units are designated to serve families at 80 percent of the area median income; the remainder are market-rate residences. The project involves multiple levels of government financing, including the city of Nashville, the Metropolitan Development and Housing Agency, the Tennessee Housing and Development Agency, the Neighborhood Reinvestment Corporation, and several private lenders.

The 1.9-acre Row 8.9n Townhomes was given its name for its location between 8th and 9th avenues north, near downtown. Everton Oglesby Architects' (formerly Everton Oglesby Askew) design for the 29 condominiums is a variation on the urban rowhouse. Units on the street are rotated 45 degrees to fit the site and create small entrance courts, while off-street units complete a parking courtyard. Constructed of brick and Hardieplank® (a high-quality, flame- and weather-resistant cement fiber siding material), the attached townhouses feature brick detailing, copper trim, accent siding, and extensive landscaping. Each unit has a deck area and private, secure parking. An interior courtyard provides communal green space.

The project's loft-style units range from 930 square feet to 1,220 square feet. All are two- or three-bedroom townhouse units. Open, sunlit floor plans emphasize the height of the dwellings. On the Eighth Avenue side, the lofts overlooking the angled two-story living spaces capture the view to the state capitol. Ninth Avenue units are oriented more toward the street. The design carefully considers the connection between the new units and the existing neighborhood, and large windows provide the eyes on the street that increase homeowners' feelings of security.

One of the project's notable features is the small difference between subsidized homes and market-rate homes. All the units are furnished with maple cabinets, sisal and Berber carpets, stainless steel appliances, and oak floors. Although a bit more expensive, these high-quality features have helped to attract everyone from young professionals to empty nesters to the project and create a strong sense of ownership among the residents.

This project has been a great success in terms of creating a market demand and reducing crime. The demand for the project was so high that 24 of the 29 units were sold before the project was completed. The project's success has encouraged the same development team to build a similar project just down the street. The drastic changes to Hope Gardens and the difference that Row 8.9n has made led the U.S. Department of Housing and Urban Development to name it a 2003 winner in the 20th annual Best in American Living competition.

AHR financed the $6.08 million project through a combination of state, local, and private channels. The firm's reputation alone enabled it to secure the $3.75 million needed for construction costs from traditional lenders, although there was concern during the search for financing that the project would fail. Putting market-rate homes in an area that had traditionally been a high-crime, low-income neighborhood seemed risky to some, but all units, affordable and market rate, sold before construction was completed.

DEVELOPMENT TEAM

Developer
Affordable Housing Resources, Inc.
Nashville, Tennessee

Architect
Everton Oglesby Architects
Nashville, Tennessee

Landscape Architect
Hawkins Partners, Inc.
Nashville, Tennessee

Everton Oglesby Architects

RESIDENTS

Area Median Income (family of 4)	$58,300
Residents Served	38% of units serve those at 80% of AMI

LAND USE INFORMATION

Site Area	1.9 acres
Total Dwelling Units	29
Gross Project Density	15.3 units per acre
Housing Type	Rowhouse

RESIDENTIAL UNIT INFORMATION

Unit Type	Floor Area (Sq. Ft.)	No. Built	Sale Price
1-Bedroom/Loft/2.5-Bath	1,220	8	$165,000–$170,000
1-Bedroom/Loft/1.5-Bath	1,160	2	$130,000
1-Bedroom/Loft/1.5-Bath	1,150	8	$130,000
1-Bedroom/Loft/1.5-Bath	930	1	$115,000
2- or 3-Bedroom/2.5-Bath	1,160	10	$130,000

FUNDING SOURCES

Source	Amount	% of Total
City of Nashville		
Tax Increment Financing, Nashville Housing Fund	$1,300,000	21
Urban Development Action Grant Repayments	350,000	6
State of Tennessee		
Tennessee Housing Development Agency HOME Funds	480,000	8
Other Sources		
Calvert Foundation (equity)	150,000	2
Neighborhood Reinvestment Corporation (capital investment for predevelopment)	50,000	1
Construction Financing	3,750,000	62
Total	**$6,080,000**	**100**

DEVELOPMENT COSTS

Development Cost Information	Amount	% of Total
Site Acquisition	$700,000	12
Site Improvement/Construction	3,750,000	62
Public Improvements	880,000	14
Total Soft Costs	750,000	12
Total	**$6,080,000**	**100**

Everton Oglesby Architects

Silicon Valley's meteoric economic boom in the 1990s raised fortunes for many, but in its wake came exorbitant housing prices and a crisis in affordable housing. Especially hard hit were those at the lower end of the economic spectrum. In 1996, just as the economy was starting to take off, the average monthly rent in the region was $1,124, and the average vacancy rate was only 2.5 percent. At its height, monthly rent in the area averaged $1,950, accompanied by a vacancy rate of 0.6 percent.

One of the groups hardest hit by the skyrocketing rents was the developmentally disabled. The state of California considers "developmental disability" an umbrella term referring to the presence of certain conditions that can include mental retardation, cerebral palsy, and autism with onset before 18 years of age. Nationwide, housing options for people with developmental disabilities are very limited. Most live in group homes or at home with parents or other family.

The developmentally disabled have very few opportunities to live independently. According to the Housing Choices Coalition, an organization that helps to secure housing for the developmentally disabled, the main reason so few opportunities exist is that the developmentally disabled have limited financial resources. The unemployment rate among persons with all types of disabilities is a staggering 70 percent. The main source of income for many developmentally disabled individuals is Social Security benefits, and in Santa Clara County, the average rent for a one-bedroom apartment is in most instances higher than a developmentally disabled person's income.

With some of the most rapidly rising housing prices in the nation during the dot-com boom, the developmentally disabled in Silicon Valley experienced a major housing crisis. One social service provider for the developmentally disabled, HOPE Rehabilitation, noted that 30 percent of its clients had to leave a work training center because they could not find local housing.

In 1996, Charities Housing Development Corporation, an affordable housing provider affiliated with Catholic Charities, decided to address this need. Working with the Housing Choices Coalition, Charities Housing started a development project that would later become Stoney Pine Affordable Housing for the Developmentally Disabled.

One of the biggest obstacles the development team faced was the acquisition of land. The development team had found a parcel that was well suited to its needs, but the owners were not interested in selling, but wanted a long-term lease that would generate a steady revenue for years to come. A series of meetings over a 14-month period convinced the owners to sell the property to Stoney Pine, even though they had received other offers on the property at substantially higher prices. This warm relationship between buyer and seller continued even after the property was sold: the sellers were present at both the groundbreaking and the grand opening ceremonies for the housing project.

Funding for the project came from a wide range of sources but primarily from the HUD Section 811 Capital Advance Program and the city of Sunnyvale. Competition for Section 811 funds is very tight, as funds are available for only a meager 40 units a year for the HUD San Francisco Multifamily Hub, an area that covers 46 counties in northern and central California. The success in securing these funds speaks to the dire need for this type of housing in Silicon Valley as well as to the high levels of community support spanning local government, private businesses, and residents.

Despite support from the city of Sunnyvale, some entitlement challenges still existed. Although the parcel was zoned for high-density residential, allowing up to 31 units or 35 dwelling units per acre on site, the city council at the time was very wary about high densities. Close negotiations with city council members, the mayor, and various city staff led to an arrangement in which Charities Housing agreed to build eight fewer units, or 26 dwelling units per acre. In return, the city offered to provide additional financial support for the project.

Further complicating the development process were the rapidly increasing costs of construction. As the real estate market heated up, it became increasingly difficult to find both contractors and construction supplies. Contractors, who needed more money to maintain a crew on site, considered the federal Davis-Bacon wage determinants (prevailing wage rates to be paid on federally funded or assisted construction projects) too low. The building boom also created a constant shortage of construction supplies. To save money, a contractor was selected early on to provide input on construction methods and materials. Even after such cost-saving measures, the bids came in at 20 percent over budget.

The design was changed until the budget shortfall was reduced by half. Through such budgetary scrutiny, extensive fundraising efforts, and a willingness to work with the city, the city of Sunnyvale approved payment of additional funds needed to close the construction loans and start the construction.

Completed in 2001, Stoney Pine now provides homes for 32 people in 23 units, including the resident manager, who is an employee of Charities Housing. The project serves residents whose income is less than 50 percent of the area median income. Monthly rent is based on 30 percent of each resident's income, no matter how small.

Designed by the architectural firm David Baker + Partners, Stoney Pine consists of three residential buildings and one community building grouped around an interior courtyard with a covered arcade connecting the structures. The community building opens onto this common area through a great door, allowing activities to expand into the courtyard. This door can be transformed into a large movie screen so that residents can view films outdoors during warm summer evenings. Carports and surface parking provide 27 parking spaces, a ratio of 1.17 spaces per unit.

The three residential buildings house one-, two-, and three-bedroom apartments in two-story wood frame structures on concrete foundations. Use of color and massing gives the project a small, noninstitutional scale. Direct input from some developmentally disabled individuals helped the designers plan the amenities for each dwelling: ceiling light fixtures, a refrigerator, a gas range, and gas-fired electric-ignition wall heaters. Each unit also has a microwave oven.

DEVELOPMENT TEAM

Developer
Charities Housing Development Corp.
San Jose, California

Architect
David Baker + Partners
San Francisco, California

Builder
Agresti & Associates
Santa Clara, California

Color Consultant
Shift Design Studio
San Francisco, California

Area Median Income (family of 4)	$105,500
Residents Served	100% of units serve the developmentally disabled who earn less than 50% of AMI

Site Area	0.9 acre
Total Dwelling Units	23
Gross Project Density	26 units per acre
Parking Total	27
Parking Ratio	1.17
Housing Type	Apartments

Unit Type	Floor Area (Sq. Ft.)	No. Built	Rent (30% of Tenant's Income)
1-Bedroom/1-Bath	525	12	$181–789
2-Bedroom/1-Bath	736	8	$138–792
3-Bedroom/1.5-Bath	955	2	$325–786
3-Bedroom/1.5-Bath	1,050	1	$594

Development Cost Information	Amount	% of Total
Site Acquisition	$1,197,600	24
Site Improvement/Construction		
General Requirements	175,300	4
Site Work	412,900	8
Structures	2,004,400	40
Overhead and Profit	171,800	3
Public Improvements	221,800	4
Soft Costs		
Architecture/Engineering	266,000	5
Relocation	159,800	3
Permit Fees	138,500	3
Miscellaneous	211,500	4
Total	**$4,959,600**	**100**

Source	Amount	% of Total
HUD Section 811 Capital Advance Program	$2,275,900	46
City of Sunnyvale		
Community Development Block Grants	525,000	11
HOME	780,000	16
Housing Mitigation Funds	420,000	8
County of Santa Clara		
Community Development Block Grants	300,000	6
Housing Bond Trust Fund	100,000	2
City of Mountain View		
Community Development Block Grants	9,000	0
HOME	115,000	2
City of Santa Clara		
HOME	100,000	2
Federal Home Loan Bank Affordable Housing Program	90,000	2
Various Grants	226,400	5
Miscellaneous Income	18,200	0
Total	**$4,959,500**	**100**

David Baker + Partners

Across the country, cities have begun to push for increased downtown residential units, hoping to reinvigorate once-thriving areas. Many cities see the creation of a 24-hour downtown as the key to successful urban regeneration, at the center of which is an increased number of residential units and the facilities and infrastructure to lure residents back downtown. Like most cities across the country, Oakland experienced middle-class flight and the abandonment of its urban residential core. The city of Oakland has begun to encourage developers to build new residential units in the city center. Initial efforts have focused on three blocks of the city's former commercial district, Old Oakland, including the former site of Swan's Market.

Swan's Market once served as the market for a large portion of Oakland. Originally constructed in 1917, Swan's Market expanded over the next 23 years; by 1940, it occupied the entire city block. But by 1984, nearly all tenants had left, the building closed, and it fell into disrepair. For 14 years, the building lay vacant until the city began to push for the redevelopment of Old Oakland; the East Bay Asian Local Development Corporation (EBALDC) took on the task of redeveloping the property in 1998.

Because of the building's historic status, EBALDC and its project partner, Pyatok Architects, were forced to take an unusual approach to developing the buildings. By implementing a mixed-use, mixed-income scheme, EBALDC managed to preserve 75 percent of the building's original structure while creating a highly successful residential and commercial development.

Even with its history of building high-quality affordable housing throughout the East Bay area, EBALDC encountered new challenges with the Swan's Market project. The city of Oakland's plan for the Old Oakland neighborhood did not include any affordable units; the city had hoped to build strictly market-rate units. EBALDC was forced to take its case to the city and after much debate convinced officials to accept the proposal that included affordable units. The city would not agree to all units' being affordable, however, which resulted in EBALDC's developing its first market-rate units.

When completed in 2000, Swan's Market contained 38 units—18 affordable units renting at between $199 and $760 and 20 cohousing condominiums. It also included 52,000 square feet of retail and office space. Because of the required market-rate portion of the building, EBALDC decided to partner with the Cohousing Company to develop the condominiums and 3,500-square-foot common house. The cohousing also created an interesting funding opportunity. As potential residents became interested in the project, a group of investors who saw its financial potential contributed a considerable amount of funding to the project.

During building and renovation, 25 percent of the building had to be removed for the addition of a larger two-story structure containing ground-floor retail space and affordable apartments above. This new structure created a seamless, fluid facade with the rest of the building. By removing the roof and leaving portions of the support beams exposed, a 5,000-square-foot open-air court was created that acts as the heart of the development. A popular destination for residents and shoppers alike, the central court hosts regular farmers' markets, impromptu performances, and numerous other activities throughout the year. With many shops, restaurants, galleries, and a museum located on the court, the open space facilitates community interaction and helps to fosters community identity. Residential units, all of which are located on the second floor, have access to the open areas through an outdoor walkway. Together, it allows shoppers and residents alike to mingle and discover the appeal of Swan's Market.

Because of Swan's Market's unique position as an adaptive use and affordable housing development, the opportunity for creative financing existed. As a result of the 1986 Tax Act, California, like most other states, offers developers incentives to build affordable housing units in the form of LIHTCs. But in California especially, competition for these tax credits has reached unprecedented levels, forcing some developers to plan creative new developments that look to improve the entire community to make their projects stand out to decision makers. Developers no longer can afford to build strictly low-income, block-style housing. Swan's Market thus includes many of the features that developers try to include in their creative developments. EBALDC applied for and received LIHTCs to fund the 18 affordable housing units. As part of the agreement, Swan's Market's affordable units are set aside for individuals earning up to 60 percent of the area median income, with some units marked for people earning from 35 to 40 percent of the area median. Additionally, some for-sale units had been marked for affordable housing, but because of the high cost of housing, those units were returned to market-rate units.

These tax credits cannot be applied to market-rate or commercial developments, so EBALDC was forced to look elsewhere for the money to complete the project. A fraction of the commercial/retail portion of development costs was covered by historic preservation tax credits as a result of the adaptive use of the buildings. Other financing came from more traditional routes, such as Alameda County, Citibank, Fannie Mae, and the Old Oakland Residence Group. Altogether, EBALDC raised $20 million for the project.

DEVELOPMENT TEAM

Developer
East Bay Asian Local Development Corporation
Oakland, California

Architect
Pyatok Architects, Inc.
Oakland, California

DEVELOPMENT COSTS

Development Cost Information	Amount	% of Total
Total Construction Hard Costs	$ 11,754,300	45
Total Tenant Improvement Budget	3,314,800	13
Total Soft Costs		0
Architectural Fees	1,130,600	4
Legal	132,700	1
Survey, Construction Testing, and Soils	178,800	1
Permits, Fees, and Utilities	567,200	2
Construction Loan Interest	530,400	2
Construction Loan Origination Fee and Bond Premium	214,300	1
Bridge Loan Fees, Expenses, and CoHousing Interest	109,400	0
Taxes (including Transfer Tax)	110,900	0
Insurance, Title, and Recording	168,000	1
Marketing and Vacancy Loss	105,000	0
Broker's Fees	157,800	1
Other Consultant Expenses	294,500	1
Project Reserves (deferred)	310,700	1
Capital Campaign Fundraising	275,000	1
Administrative Expenses, Fees, and Overhead	1,001,500	4
Business Training and Marketing in Retail	114,000	0
Soft Cost Subtotal	5,400,900	21
Total	**$25,870,800**	**100**

Pyatok Architects, Inc.

Area Median Income (family of 4)	$76,600
Residents Served	64% of units serve those at 30% of AMI

LAND USE INFORMATION

Site Area	One city block
Total Dwelling Units	38
Total Parking	35 spaces
Parking Ratio	1.1 for cohousing. Rentable by residents of affordable units.
Housing Type	Multifamily

RESIDENTIAL UNIT INFORMATION

Unit Type	No. Built	Rent (1st Month)
1- and 2-Bedroom Rentals	18	$199–760
Cohousing	20	N/A

Pyatok Architects, Inc.

FUNDING SOURCES

Source	Amount	% of Total
Cohousing		
Wells Fargo	$2,810,000	11
Old Oakland Group LLC	315,000	1
ORA	750,000	3
Proceeds from Sales	675,000	3
Rental Housing		
Wells Fargo	1,561,800	6
Fannie Mae PRI Loan	200,000	1
Oakland Redevelopment Agency	600,000	2
Alameda County HCD	500,000	2
AHP Grant (CitiBank)	90,000	0
Fannie Mae and Other Grants	165,000	1
CHFA Tax Credit Bridge Loan	730,000	3
CHFA	775,000	3
CHFA HAT Loan	240,000	1
CEF Tax Credit Purchase	1,350,000	5
Commercia/Retail		
Wells Fargo	3,350,000	13
Oakland Redevelopment Agency	1,150,000	4
HHS OCS Grant	500,000	2
EDA Grant	1,700,000	6
Prepaid Rents for Tenant Improvements	1,700,000	6
Capital Campaign Donations	1,150,000	4
StanCorp Mortgage Investors	3,500,000	13
Foundation PRI Loan	300,000	1
Historic Tax Credits	2,200,000	8
Total	**$26,311,800**	**100**

Pyatok Architects, Inc.

Migrant farmworkers all across America endure housing unthinkable to most of us. Many times, farmworkers camp out in parking lots, sleeping in their cars if they are fortunate. The less fortunate sleep outside with only sheets of cardboard or old mattresses between them and the ground. Further, when farmworkers rent housing, they are often able to afford only substandard and often dangerous housing.

A 2001 study conducted by the Housing Assistance Council (HAC) on the conditions of housing for farmworkers across the United States found that 17 percent live in severely substandard housing and another 16 percent live in moderately substandard housing. In comparison, the 1997 American Housing Survey (AHS) found that only 5 percent of all American households live in moderately substandard housing and only 2 percent live in severely substandard housing. The HAC study further found that 19 percent of the substandard housing units for farmworkers inflict a heavy cost burden on their residents, who typically must pay more than 30 percent of their income for that housing.

How substandard are these housing units? According to HAC, 10 percent lack a working stove, 8 percent lack a bath or shower, 9 percent lack a toilet, 43 percent lack a telephone, and 52 percent lack access to laundry facilities. Structural problems such as sagging roofs or house frames affected 22 percent of the units, 15 percent had holes in the roof or were missing large patches of shingles, 36 percent had broken glass or screens in the windows or doors, 29 percent suffered water damage, and 19 percent had unsanitary conditions such as rodent or insect infestation. The problems of substandard housing are especially acute for children, with 65 percent of both moderately and severely substandard units occupied by children.

As in the rest of the nation, housing conditions for farmworkers in Center, Colorado, were not very good. This small community in Colorado's San Luis Valley relies heavily on agriculture, producing potatoes, alfalfa, lettuce, barley, and carrots. To improve housing conditions and overall quality of life for the farmworkers and their families, the Colorado Rural Housing Development Corporation, working with the U.S. Department of Agriculture Rural Development Program, built Tierra Nueva, Phase II. Phase I of the development consists of three dormitories for single male migrant workers.

Although funding for Phase II came from a combination of public and private sources, the majority came from a U.S. Department of Agriculture Farm Labor Housing grant for $2.5 million. The USDA also provides rental assistance to residents, with the stipulation that occupants must derive at least one-third of their income from farm labor. In the winter, when the migrant farmworkers have moved on, the units are rented to other homeless families.

The 29,150-square-foot Phase II addition of Tierra Nueva makes it one of the largest housing projects for farmworkers in the nation. Phase II provides five buildings with a total of 25 townhouses designed for families. Along with the 16 two-story three-bedroom units and nine one-story four-bedroom units, the developers also built a community center that includes a computer lab, office and meeting space, and a Head Start school program for the children. The Head Start school provides educational, health, and social services to children between six weeks and kindergarten age.

Faleide Architects's primary philosophy guiding the design of the townhouses was that people should feel at home where they live. Their houses therefore create a strong sense of place, in turn engendering a sense of security, warmth, family, and community that helps shape residents' values and interactions.

Photos: Faleide Architects, PC

Every dwelling has its own private entrance and porch, giving each one a sense of arrival. The homes are situated so that they clearly belong to both the new community center and the nearby public green space. The architects used related colors and similar forms, along with a traffic loop, to enhance the sense of connection between the two phases of the project.

Ingenious use of low-cost, low-maintenance materials such as vinyl windows, cement fiber siding, and asphalt shingles, and concrete crawl-space foundations help this project balance pragmatism with a sense of stylish domesticity. Another important design feature is the use of regional iconic and symbolic imagery found throughout the San Luis Valley to give a sense of connection with the larger Center, Colorado, community and to create a sense of commonality and unity within the project.

Faleide Architects, PC

DEVELOPMENT TEAM

Developer
San Luis Valley Farm Worker Housing, Inc.
Center, Colorado

Architect
Faleide Architects, PC
Denver, Colorado

Builder
High Country Builders

Funder
Colorado Rural Housing and Development Corporation
Westminster, Colorado

RESIDENTS

Area Median Income (family of 4)	$40,200
Median Income for Farmworkers	$10,000
Residents Served	20% of units serve those at 50% of AMI

LAND USE INFORMATION

Site Area	4.5 acres
Total Dwelling Units	25
Gross Project Density	5.6 units per acre
Housing Type	4-bedroom flats and 3-bedroom townhouses

RESIDENTIAL UNIT INFORMATION

Unit Type	No. Built	Rent (1st Month)
3-Bedroom/2-Bath Duplex	16	$575

FUNDING SOURCES

Source	Amount	% of Total
USDA 1% Loan	$725,100	27
USDA Grant	1,774,900	65
Federal Home Loan Bank of Topeka	100,000	4
Neighborhood Reinvestment	125,000	4
Total	**$2,725,000**	**100**

DEVELOPMENT COSTS

Development Cost Information	Amount	% of Total
Land	$20,000	0.7
Soils Test	5,800	0.2
Building Permit	14,000	0.5
Construction	2,271,700	83.4
Off-Site Costs	20,000	0.7
Architect	115,000	4.2
Engineer	15,100	0.6
Construction Insurance	10,000	0.4
Construction Interest	10,000	0.4
Developer/Technical Assistance	89,000	3.3
Loan Fees	6,000	0.2
Operating Reserves	44,600	1.7
Market Study	4,500	0.2
Furnishings	99,300	3.6
Total	**$2,725,000**	**100.0**

Faleide Architects, PC

TOWNHOMES ON CAPITOL HILL   WASHINGTON, D.C.   1998

Until 1996, the degradation of U.S. public housing policy was easily illustrated with a telephoto shot of the U.S. Capitol dome, framed by the shells of abandoned public housing on Capitol Hill. Today, that vista no longer exists, least of all from the doorsteps of the Townhomes on Capitol Hill, a residential development that blends into the surrounding neighborhood of elegant Victorian and Federal-style townhouses.

Capitol Hill is a mixed-income, richly diverse neighborhood of approximately 50,000 residents and two major commercial corridors. If the National Mall forms the Capitol's front lawn, Capitol Hill is its backyard, starting immediately east of the U.S. Capitol, Supreme Court, and Library of Congress buildings. Since its earliest days as a rural village, the neighborhood has been home to workers associated with the government: congressional representatives, staffers, lobbyists, and Navy Yard workers.

In 1940, the government built an 18-building public housing complex of garden apartments in a mix of rowhouses and apartment blocks, seven blocks southeast of the Capitol. It was named the Ellen Wilson Dwellings, after the wife of President Woodrow Wilson, whose deathbed wish was to abolish substandard housing. In the early 1970s, the elevated Southeast Freeway was built, cutting off a corner of the block where the complex was located. As a result, the surrounding area became an isolated and dead-end edge of its neighborhood. Finally in 1988, with a plan to renovate the buildings and return its 129 displaced households, city public housing officials closed the complex. But the city never rehabilitated the property. A judgment against the city in a 1992 lawsuit filed by families on the city's waiting list for public housing led to the city housing authority's being placed under federal receivership, throwing all plans into further chaos.

The Ellen Wilson Dwellings became a haven for drug dealers, drug users, and squatters, traumatizing neighbors and threatening their property values. Not wanting to wait for the cash-strapped city to keep its promise, in 1990 the neighborhood formed a community development corporation (CDC) to redevelop the site. The CDC brought in Telesis, a local developer of affordable housing, and Corcoran Jennison, a Boston-based development, marketing, and management firm, to implement a novel proposal: a limited-equity cooperative where residents would buy a share in the development and pay a monthly fee. This plan would allow lower-income families to own property with lower-than-conventional downpayments and monthly payments that would be partially subsidized by higher-income families. Under the HOPE VI program, the U.S. Department of Housing and Urban Development issued a $25 million grant for construction.

HOPE VI funding requires that residents have low to moderate incomes. It also requires that the CDC work closely with tenants and the community in its development strategy. Thus, the CDC was faced with finding a balance between attracting enough higher-income families to offset the lower co-op fees of low-income families, while assuaging its gentrified community that was split on the issue of attracting new residents who could afford market-rate housing and attracting back displaced former neighbors with low incomes. The solution was to use a banded-ownership formula and to architecturally meld the project into its neighborhood.

Hoachlander Davis Photography, LLC

Of the 134 new units on the 5.3-acre site, 34 are reserved for households with incomes below 25 percent of the area median income, 33 for households between 25 and 50 percent of the median, and 67 for households between 50 and 115 percent. Downpayments—in the parlance of co-op ownership, "share prices"—are as high as three times the monthly fee, and co-op fees are based on the home value and income band of the unit owner. These monthly payments cover all operating expenses and the reserve. HUD's $25 million grant covered all capital costs up front, eliminating the need for debt service on the property. As a result, Townhomes on Capitol Hill will be maintained for 40 years without any ongoing public housing subsidies of any kind. This self-sustaining system saved taxpayers more than $34 million in housing subsidies.

HOPE VI funding requires that the developer give displaced public housing families priority in the new project. At Townhomes on Capitol Hill, only 11 households were able to return—partly because 11 years had elapsed since the diaspora, partly because of the high financial bar for co-op ownership, and partly because of the strict criteria households must meet in terms of fitness as tenants and financial credit.

The key architectural decision was to make the buildings indistinguishable from the prevalent Victorian-style townhouses of the neighborhood. Thus, houses are of similar sizes and materials on a new street grid that extends through the 5.3-acre site, creating two new streets. The intended overall effect is that the end of the neighborhood is indistinguishable from where the "project" begins. It also means that the lowest-priced townhouses have the same character and feel as the highest-priced ones, with the entire range intermixed on the same street.

The CDC retained Amy Weinstein & Associates, a Washington, D.C.–based architecture firm that—working with a public housing budget—used only five building types but achieved a seemingly infinite variety of facades and interiors by varying the use of the limited palette of building materials, fixtures, and colors. Most townhouses have two bedrooms and two bathrooms and an English-basement rental unit. The higher-priced townhouses offer three bedrooms.

To newcomers and old-time residents alike, Capitol Hill is a small town, engendering loyalty to the neighborhood above all other communally held values. One does not simply move to Capitol Hill—one joins the community. Townhomes on Capitol Hill has been embraced and its returning families welcomed back, while tourists are unaware that they are in the midst of a public housing project.

Developer
Ellen Wilson Community Development Corporation
Washington, D.C.

Architect
Amy Weinstein & Associates
Washington, D.C.

Builder
CorJen Construction
Boston, Massachusetts

Landscape Architect
Oehme, van Sweden and Associates, Inc.
Washington, D.C.

Area Median Income (family of 4)	$84,800
Residents Served	30% of units serve those at 50% of AMI; 25% of units serve those at less than 25% of AMI; 25% of units serve those at 20–50% of AMI; 50% of units serve those at 50–115% of AMI

Housing Types	36 facade designs, 5 building types mixing rowhouses and semi-detached homes; 1-, 2-, and 3-bedroom units
Number of Units	134

Hoachlander Davis Photography, LLC

Located at the crest of a hill in Los Angeles, Waterloo Heights Apartments addresses the affordable housing needs of an often forgotten population: individuals with special needs. Special-needs housing seldom offers the opportunity for independent living; rather, it offers institutional-style living at worst and group housing at best. A need exists for low-cost housing that meets the needs of its tenants but does not impede them from living a complete and independent life. This is the goal of Waterloo Heights Apartments.

Targeting those with disabilities, individuals living with AIDS, seniors, and disabled veterans, the Hollywood Community Housing Corporation (HCHC) set out to build a low-cost aesthetically pleasing development in a quiet residential neighborhood with views of downtown. Despite initial frustration and objection by neighbors, developers overcame NIMBYism by conducting regular meetings with area stakeholders and coming to an understanding about the development and its goals and design. Area residents were wary of the development from the onset because of a failed attempt to establish drug and alcohol treatment programs in the area. Additional concerns arose about the density of the development; 18 units on just over 0.4 acre might cause congestion and disrupt the serenity of the neighborhood. Despite protests over these issues, the neighbors were assured that safety concerns would be addressed and precautions would be in place in case of incidents. An on-site manager would be able to address any problems as they arose. Further, developers informed neighbors that Waterloo Heights did not approach maximum density allowances and that another developer could easily come in and build more than the 18 units proposed by Hollywood Community Housing.

The 18-unit, two-level building, which has been designed to fit into the surrounding craftsman-style neighborhood, is completely accessible to the handicapped. The architects at Koning Eizenberg Architecture managed to use the natural topography of the site to allow for the two levels, despite lacking an elevator. Floor levels step down as a result of the gradual slope yet no accessibility is lost. Using stucco and wood, the ten units along the front elevation are designed to look like a cluster of larger homes that blend in with surrounding residences. Trellises with climbing vines soften the lines. Developers were also able to include a landscaped courtyard that acts as a social center for the development. The courtyard allows for interaction between residents if they want it but also allows residents to avoid the courtyard so that no socialization is forced. Units include patios or balconies.

Financed through various government sources, development for Waterloo Heights cost $2.7 million. Most of this cost was covered by a grant from the U.S. Department of Housing and Urban Development. The remaining funds came from a combination of sources, including the Los Angeles Housing Department, City of Industry funds, and an affiliate loan from HCHC. The completed project of 18 units includes ten one-bedroom units and seven efficiency units, all priced at $315 per month for individuals with special needs whose income is less than 30 percent of the area median (the manager's apartment is included in the total count).

RESIDENTS

Area Median Income (family of 4)	$50,300
Residents Served	100% of units serve those at 30% of AMI

LAND USE INFORMATION

Site Area	0.43 acre
Total Dwelling Units	18
Gross Project Density	41 units per acre
Housing Type	Efficiency and 1-bedroom multifamily

RESIDENTIAL UNIT INFORMATION

Unit Type	Floor Area (Sq. Ft.)	No. Built	Rent (1st Month)
Studio	415	7	$315
1-Bedroom	540	10	$315
Manager's 1-Bedroom	540	1	$331

FUNDING SOURCES

Source	Amount	% of Total
Los Angeles Housing Department	$400,000	14
City of Industry Funds	867,700	31
HUD	1,365,200	50
Affiliate Loan from HCHC	119,100	4
Total	**$2,752,000**	**100**

DEVELOPMENT COSTS

Development Cost Information	Amount	% of Total
Site Acquisition	$310,000	11
General Conditions	152,200	6
Demolition/Excavation	12,400	0
Construction	781,800	28
Finishes	149,600	5
Specialties, Cabinets, Equipment, Appliances	54,000	2
HVAC	53,200	2
Plumbing/Sewers	144,100	5
Fire Protection	52,700	2
Electrical	87,500	3
Elevators	44,000	2
Landscaping	59,800	2
Public Improvements	17,600	1
Total Soft Costs	832,900	30
Total	**$2,751,800**	**100**

Lucy Gonzalez

Developer
Hollywood Community Housing Corporation
Hollywood, California

Architect and Landscape Architect
Koning Eizenberg Architecture
Santa Monica, California

Builder
Westport Construction
Arcadia, California

Lucy Gonzaez

Downtown Portsmouth, Virginia, is coming back to life. Until the 1960s, this traditional downtown was the civic and social center for the community. People came to shop and socialize. But like the rest of America, shifting development patterns led to the decline of Portsmouth's downtown. It became undervalued and underused while local residents fled to shopping malls and suburban housing developments.

In response, civic leaders embarked on a program to reverse the trend and bring downtown back to life. A vital element of their program was the destruction of the Ida Barbour housing project. Just a few blocks from downtown, the project consisted of 663 units grouped in identical two-story barracks-like buildings scattered over more than 40 acres of land.

The placement of the buildings and their relationships to the few streets that passed through the project created a series of poorly defined and unmanageable open spaces. The open spaces decreased the sense of ownership and control among residents and provided many excellent hiding places for criminals. As a result, drug use and other illegal activities became common-place. The design also made it ten to 20 times more expensive to provide police and social services than in other neighborhoods of similar size. Ida Barbour's reputation was so bad that the housing values in surrounding neighborhoods were affected by the project's terrible conditions.

Years of substandard maintenance led to estimates of $40 million to $50 million to repair the project. Yet this estimate did not include the costs needed to address the design elements that created many of the social problems experienced by the project. By 1988, the project's owner, the Portsmouth Redevelopment and Housing Authority (PRHA) wanted the project to be torn down and replaced.

In 1997, PRHA received a $24.8 million HOPE VI grant. Local and other federal funding sources then matched this amount. With $50 million in funding, PRHA sought to create a high-quality mixed-income neighborhood that would build off the demand for downtown housing as well as serve the needs of low-income citizens.

Westbury now sits on the original site of the Ida Barbour housing project. It features a variety of building types and architectural styles that honor the city's historic homes: vibrantly colored craftsman, Victorian, and Colonial revival styles, each enhanced by historically inspired porches, eaves, windows, and trim. More important, the homes occupy lots on traditional urban-style inter-connected blocks and streets with parks and squares.

Designed by Urban Design Associates, the master plan for the site comprises 539 units developed in four main phases. Of this total, 278 units are earmarked for families earning no more than 80 percent of the area median income. Of the total, 161 units are single-family detached houses and two- and three-unit attached townhouses. A series of small six-unit apartment buildings contains the 117 rental units, which are split between public housing (primarily taxpayer financed) and subsidized units. All dwellings feature value-engineered low-maintenance construction, energy-saving utilities, and numerous modern amenities.

A continuous park system provides recreation areas. Residential blocks follow the traditional pattern of tree-lined streets and service alleys. Each block contains a combination of rental and homeownership units, representing a variety of income levels.

A major amenity is Westbury's wireless Internet infrastructure. In 2001, Westbury became one of the first wireless communities in the nation.

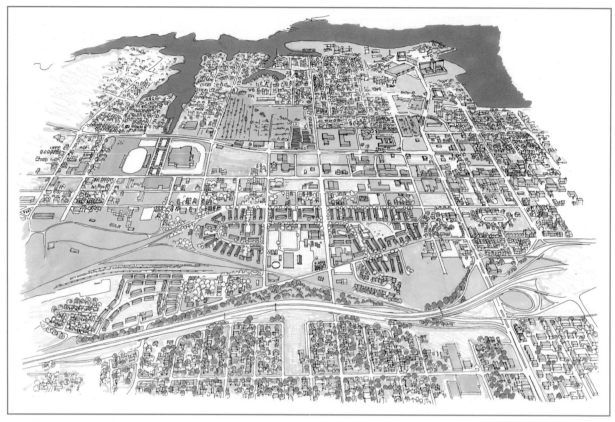

Urban Design Associates

Urban Design Associates

DEVELOPMENT TEAM

Developer
Portsmouth Housing and Redevelopment Authority
Portsmouth, Virginia

Architect
Urban Design Associates
Pittsburgh, Pennsylvania

Builder
Woodbury Construction
Chesapeake, Virginia

Landscape Architect
LaQuatra Bonci Associates
Pittsburgh, Pennsylvania

Area Median Income (family of 4)	$55,200
Residents Served	100% of units serve those at 80% of AMI

LAND USE INFORMATION

Site Area	41.4 acres
Total Dwelling Units	278
Gross Project Density	6.7 units per acre
Housing Type	161 single-family detached houses; 2- and 3-unit attached townhouses; 117 rental units housed in a series of small 6-unit apartment buildings

RESIDENTIAL UNIT INFORMATION

Unit Type	Floor Area (Sq. Ft.)	No. Built	Sale Price
Phase I			$90,426
32-Foot-Wide	1,536	32	$96,246
24-Foot-Wide	1,496	5	$90,800
24-Foot-Wide	1,440	11	$84,750
3-Bedroom Duplex	1,408	5	$75,529
2-Bedroom Duplex	1,152	9	
Phase II			$109,750
32-Foot-Wide	1,536	40	$104,750
24-Foot-Wide	1,496	31	$97,750
3-Bedroom Duplex	1,408	14	$86,850
2-Bedroom Duplex	1,152	14	
Rental Units			*
1-Bedroom	683	10	*
2-Bedroom	1,152	40	*
2-Bedroom	1,035	20	*
3-Bedroom	1,408	23	*
1-Bedroom	780	24	

* 30 percent of income.

FUNDING SOURCES

Source	Amount	% of Total
HOPE VI Grant	$18,684,300	34
HOPE VI Loan(s)	1,912,300	3
Tax Credit Equity	6,967,100	13
Proceeds of Sales Phase I	5,292,700	10
Proceeds of Sales Phase II	8,296,100	15
Proceeds of Sales Not Used Phase IIB	(817,500)	–1
Proceeds of Phase I Sales Used in Another Phase	2,291,200	4
Proceeds of Sales Not Used Phase I	(2,659,200)	–5
Empowerment Zone Funds	231,000	0
PHA Capital Funds	2,226,100	4
Federal Home Loan Bank Grants/IAHTF	800,000	1
CDBG Funds	1,019,200	2
City of Portsmouth CIP Funds	2,114,000	4
PRHA Replacement Factor Funds	700,000	1
HOPE VI Funds	4,214,300	8
Proceeds of Phase I Sales	1,003,600	2
Proceeds of Phase II Sales	938,200	2
PHA Capital Funds	2,097,100	4
CDBG Funds	64,800	0
Washington Park Demolition Hope VI Funds	175,000	0
Total	**$55,550,300**	**100**

DEVELOPMENT COSTS

Development Cost Information	Amount	% of Total
Site Acquisition	$1,050,500	2
Site Improvement/Construction	6,100,000	11
General Conditions	1,176,100	2
Demolition/Excavation	2,046,700	4
Construction	21,745,100	39
Relocation	793,400	1
Community and Support Services	3,616,100	7
Environmental Remediation	1,256,500	2
Architecture	1,284,800	2
Engineering	1,381,400	2
Accounting	87,700	0
Legal	588,000	1
Permit Fees	580,000	1
Consultants	1,254,100	2
Developer's Fee	3,071,500	6
Construction Management	994,400	2
Other Soft Costs	8,523,900	15
Total	**$55,550,300**	**100**

Amenity
Nonmonetary tangible or intangible benefit derived from real property often offered to a lessee, typically recreational facilities, concierge services, or planned activities.

AMI
Area median income, as calculated by the federal government and adjusted for household size and local cost of living.

Attached housing
Two or more dwelling units constructed with party walls (townhouses or stacked flats, for example).

Building code
Rules established by local governments that dictate the standards to which buildings must be constructed. Building codes are intended to make the structure safer and more resistant to failure. Older buildings may need repairs and new construction to conform to modern building codes.

Capital
Money or property invested in an asset for the creation of wealth; alternatively, the surplus of production over consumption.

Central business district (CBD)
The center of commercial activity in a town or city; usually the largest and oldest concentration of such activity.

Closing costs
Also referred to as *settlement costs,* these costs are paid at loan closing and may include prepaid interest (points), attorney's fees, title insurance, and inspections.

Cohousing
A form of collaborative housing intended to provide the benefits of homeownership within a tightly knit community. The most common configuration is 20 to 30 single-family homes clustered around a pedestrian street or courtyard. The community usually has recreational facilities, libraries, lounges, children's space, and a communal dining hall where residents share several meals a week.

Community development block grant (CDBG)
HUD-administered program that provides lump-sum payments to state and local governments. Funds can be used only for specific uses such as economic development, rehabilitation of historic or distressed housing, and infrastructure. State and local governments may establish their own projects and priorities as long as they meet funding criteria.

Community development corporation (CDC)
An entrepreneurial institution that combines public and private resources to aid in the development of socio-economically disadvantaged areas.

Community redevelopment agency (CRA)
An agency created by a local government to redevelop a specified area.

Condominium
A form of joint ownership and control of property in which specified volumes of airspace (for example, apartments) are owned individually and common elements of the building (for example, land, outside walls, recreational facilities) are jointly owned.

Conventional loan
Financing provided by private lenders, usually banks. Conventional loans are loans made without subsidy or assistance.

Cooperative
A form of ownership in which a purchaser buys shares of a housing cooperative rather than an individual unit. The owner then "leases back" a particular unit in the cooperative. Cooperative ownership offers some advantages over real property, including group insurance, divestiture of liability for major repairs, and a lower purchase price. Disadvantages include difficulty securing financing and renting out units.

Demographics
Information on population characteristics by location, including such aspects as age, employment, earnings, and expenditures.

Density
The level of concentration (high or low) of buildings or population within a given area. Often expressed as a ratio, for example, dwelling units per acre.

Detached housing
A freestanding dwelling unit, normally for a single family, situated on its own lot.

Developer
One who prepares raw land for improvement by installing roads, utilities, and so forth. A developer either sells lots to builders or functions as a builder, constructing structures on real estate.

Downpayment
The portion of the purchase price paid at the time of purchase. The downpayment is the difference between the sale price and the loan amount. Lenders set specific requirements for this amount, which may vary based on the type of financing.

ELI
Extremely low income. Earning less than 30 percent of the area income.

Equity
That portion of property or other securities that is owned outright, that is, above the amount financed.

Fannie Mae
Formerly the Federal National Mortgage Association or FNMA, a federal government–sponsored entity that purchases mortgage loans in the secondary market. Fannie Mae also invests in tax credit projects and provides other financing products for housing development.

Fee simple
The most extensive interest in land recognized by law. Absolute ownership but subject to the limitations of police power, taxation, eminent domain, and private restrictions of record.

Freddie Mac
Federal Home Loan Mortgage Company or FHLMC, a federal government–sponsored entity that purchases mortgage loans in the secondary market.

Garden apartments
Two- or three-story multifamily housing development that features low density, ample open space around buildings, and on-site parking.

Ginnie Mae
Government National Mortgage Association (GNMA), the federally owned secondary loan market agency. Unlike Fannie Mae or Freddie Mac, Ginnie Mae is owned by the federal government rather than private shareholders.

Ground lease
A long-term lease on a parcel of land, separate from and exclusive of the improvements on the land.

High rise
Tall building, usually more than 16 stories for office buildings or ten stories for residential buildings.

Historic tax credit
Tax incentive given to owners of properties listed on the National Register of Historic Places who substantially rehabilitate distressed historic properties. Federal tax credits are worth 20 percent of the historic property's value and reduce the owner's income tax liability dollar for dollar. Tax credits can also be sold to raise capital for rehabilitation projects.

HOME
A HUD program that provides block grants directly to local governments and states. The program is very flexible but must be used to provide for, rehabilitate, or administer local low-income housing programs.

HOPE VI
Homeownership and Opportunity for People Everywhere, a HUD-sponsored affordable housing program founded in 1992. HOPE VI provides direct funding and loans to developers. It marked a major policy shift in public housing that encourages mixed income and mixed uses in projects involving affordable units instead of isolated public housing projects. HOPE VI also promotes the upgrade and renovation of the old public housing stock.

HOPWA
Housing Opportunities for Persons with AIDS. A HUD program offering grants for states and local governments to provide housing, social services, and treatment for persons living with AIDS. Alternatively, HOPWA funds can be spent on housing for persons with mental disabilities and chemical dependency.

Housing Choice Voucher Program
Also known as "Section 8," this program provides housing vouchers to enable very low-income elderly or disabled individuals and families to afford safe, decent rental housing. These vouchers are a cash grant and do not have to be repaid.

HUD

U.S. Department of Housing and Urban Development, a Cabinet-level executive agency of the U.S. government. The agency implements programs and monitors conditions with regard to the nation's housing, growth, and urban problems.

Infrastructure

Services and facilities provided by a municipality, including roads, highways, water, sewerage, emergency services, parks and recreation, and so on. Can also be privately provided.

Joint venture

An association of two or more firms or individuals to carry on a single business enterprise for profit.

Land development

The process of preparing raw land through clearing, grading, installing utilities, and so on for the construction of improvements.

Lease

A contract that gives the lessor (the tenant) the right of possession for a period of time in return for paying rent to the lessee (the landlord).

LEED

Leadership in Energy and Environmental Design. A voluntary national standard for developing sustainable, or "green," buildings. Developers build product according to standards published by the U.S. Green Building Council, and, if it meets the standards, the end product is certified.

Lien

The right to hold property as security until the debt that it secures is paid. A mortgage is one type of lien.

Limited partnership

A partnership that restricts the personal liability of the partners to the amount of their investment.

Loan-to-value (LTV) ratio

The relationship between the amount of a mortgage loan and the value of the real estate securing it; the loan amount divided by market value.

Low income

A household whose income is 50 to 80 percent of the area median income by size. HUD and census data are used to calculate low-income limits.

Low-income housing tax credit (LIHTC).

A ten-year tax credit given as an incentive to private developers to acquire, build, or rehabilitate low-income rental units. Developers enter into a minimum 30-year, extended low-income use agreement. A percentage of dwelling units is reserved for low-income persons. The program was enacted in 1986.

Low rise

A building with one to three stories.

Mid rise

A building with four to 15 stories.

Mixed-use development

A development, in one building or several buildings, that combines at least three significant revenue-producing uses that are physically and functionally integrated and developed in conformance with a coherent plan.

Mortgage

An instrument used in some states (rather than a deed of trust) to make real estate security for a debt. A two-party instrument between a mortgagor (a borrower) and a mortgagee (a lender).

Move-up housing

Typically, larger, more expensive houses that homeowners buy as their incomes increase. First homes— "starter homes"—are generally more modest in size and price.

Multifamily housing

Structures that contain more than one housing unit. The U.S. Census Bureau considers multifamily housing to be buildings with five or more units.

Neighborhood

A segment of a city or town with common features that distinguish it from adjoining areas.

Option

The right given by the owner of property to another to purchase or lease the property at a specific price within a set time.

Planned unit development (PUD)

A zoning classification created to accommodate master-planned developments that allows mixed uses, varied housing types, and/or unconventional subdivision designs.

Property manager
An individual or firm responsible for the operation of improved real estate. Management functions include leasing and maintenance supervision.

Redevelopment
The redesign or rehabilitation of existing properties.

Rent control
Limitations imposed by state or local authorities on the amount of rent a landlord can charge in certain jurisdictions.

Scattered sites
Rather than building public housing in concentrated, isolated communities, the "scattered sites" approach develops public housing on a small scale, dispersing it in neighborhoods throughout a city so that it is undistinguishable from surrounding buildings.

Secondary market
Loans sold to new owners by the organization that originally loaned the money to the borrower. The new owners collect payments from the borrower. The original lender frees up cash to make new loans. Fannie Mae, Freddie Mac, and Ginnie Mae facilitate these transactions, in most cases purchasing and holding loans.

Section 8
See **Housing Choice Voucher Program**.

Single-family housing
A dwelling unit, either attached or detached, designed for use by one household and with direct access to a street; it does not share heating facilities or other essential building facilities with any other dwelling, although it may share one or more walls.

Subsidy
A below-market-rate loan, favorable terms, tax credits, or cash payments to homebuyers or renters from a government entity.

Tax-exempt bonds
Bonds issued and backed by the faith and credit of the issuing local government. Securities issued by a local government are exempt from federal and state income taxes.

Tax increment financing
The financing of infrastructure by issuing bonds backed by the increase in property tax receipts. Because property values increase after infrastructure is built, the difference in assessed values (and therefore revenues) before and after bond issuance becomes a dedicated stream of funds to repay the bond.

Tenant
One who rents property from another.

Tenant mix
The range of ages, incomes, and household types of tenants in a leased building or complex.

Title
Evidence of ownership of real property to indicate a person's right to possess, use, and dispose of the property.

Townhouse
Single-family attached residence separated from another by party walls, usually on a narrow lot offering small front- and backyards. Also called a rowhouse.

Transit-oriented development (TOD)
Development designed to promote the use of alternative modes of transportation. TODs are often found near rail stations or bus depots.

Very low income
A household whose income is 50 percent or less of the area median income. HUD and census data are used to determine income classification.

Zoning
Classification and regulation of land by local governments according to use categories (zones); often includes density designations as well. Development that conforms to the zoning classification is allowed; other land uses are not.

National Association
 of Counties
440 First Street, N.W.
Suite 800
Washington, DC 20001
(202) 393-6226
www.naco.org

National Association of
 Home Builders
1201 15th Street, N.W.
Washington, DC 20005
(800) 368-5242
www.nahb.com

National Association of
 Housing and
 Redevelopment Officials
630 I Street, N.W.
Washington, DC 20001
(877) 866-2476
www.nahro.org

National Association of Local
 Housing Finance Agencies
2025 M Street, N.W.
Suite 800
Washington, DC 20036
(202) 367-1197
www.nalhfa.org

National Association
 of Realtors®
430 North Michigan Avenue
Chicago, IL 60611
(800) 874-6500
www.realtor.org

National Building Museum
401 F Street, N.W.
Washington, DC 20001
(202) 272-2448
www.nbm.org

National Coalition for
 the Homeless
1012 14th Street, N.W.
Suite 600
Washington, DC 20005
(202) 737-6444
www.nationalhomeless.org

National Community
 Development Association
522 21st Street, N.W.
Suite 120
Washington, DC 20006
(202) 293-7587
www.ncdaonline.org

National Congress for
 Community Economic
 Development
1030 15th Street, N.W.
Suite 325
Washington, DC 20005
(202) 289-9020
www.ncced.org

National Council for State
 Housing Agencies
444 North Capitol Street, N.W.
Suite 438
Washington, DC 20001
(202) 624-7710
www.ncsha.org

National Housing
 Conference, Inc.
1801 K Street, N.W.
Suite M-100
Washington, DC 20006
(202) 466-2121
www.nhc.org

National Housing Trust
1101 30th Street, N.W.
Suite 400
Washington, DC 20007
(202) 333-8931
www.nhtinc.org

National League of Cities
1301 Pennsylvania Avenue, N.W.
Washington, DC 20004
(202) 626-3000
www.nlc.org

National Low-Income
 Housing Coalition
1012 14th Street, N.W.
Suite 610
Washington, DC 20005
(202) 662-1530
www.nlihc.org

National Multi Housing
 Council
1850 M Street, N.W.
Suite 540
Washington, DC 20036
(202) 974-2300
www.nmhc.org

National Trust for Historic
 Preservation
1785 Massachusetts Avenue, N.W.
Washington, DC 20036
(202) 588-6000
www.nthp.org

Neighborhood Housing
 Services of America
1970 Broadway
Suite 470
Oakland, CA 94612
(510) 832-5542
www.nhsofamerica.org

Neighborhood Reinvestment
 Corporation
1325 G Street, N.W.
Suite 800
Washington, DC 20005
(202) 220-2300
www.nw.org

U.S. Census Bureau
Housing and Household
 Economic Statistics Division
4700 Silver Hill Road
Suitland, MD 20746
(301) 763-3199
www.census.gov

U.S. Conference of Mayors
1620 I Street, N.W.
Washington, DC 20006
(202) 293-7330
www.usmayors.org

U.S. Department of
 Agriculture Rural
 Development Agency
1400 Independence Avenue, S.W.
Room 206
Washington, DC 20250
(202) 720-4581
www.rurdev.usda.gov

U.S. Department of Housing
 and Urban Development
Office of the Secretary
451 Seventh Street, S.W.
Washington, DC 20410
(202) 708-0417
www.hud.gov

U.S. General Accounting Office
Resources, Community,
 and Economic
 Development Division
441 G Street, N.W.
Washington, DC 20548
(202) 512-9824
www.gao.gov

United Way of America
701 North Fairfax Street
Alexandria, VA 22314
(703) 836-7200
www.unitedway.org

Urban Institute
2100 M Street, N.W.
Washington, DC 20037
(202) 833-7200
www.urbaninstitute.org

ULI–the Urban Land Institute
1025 Thomas Jefferson Street, N.W.
Suite 500 West
Washington, DC 20007
(202) 624-7000
www.uli.org